WRITERS AND CRITICS

A. NORM

Advi

DAVID DAICHES
C. P. SNOW

This book about Evelyn Waugh and his work is written
by a critic who is himself a writer with a deep sense of the
comic. He is, therefore, particularly interested in Waugh's
use of a comic attitude to establish a scale of values. He
surveys Waugh's comic techniques, his use of realism and
of farce, and in so doing questions many assumptions
which have been made about Waugh's attitudes to
society as they appear in his fiction. He examines in this
lively survey the contrast between the world of anarchy
and disorder and that of tradition, of seriousness and of
belief in Waugh's work.

Malcolm Bradbury lectures in English at the Univer-
sity of Birmingham, having previously held a post in the
Department of Adult Education in the University of
Hull. He was educated at the University College of
Leicester, the University of London, and Yale University.
He has written a novel *Eating People is Wrong* (1959) and
two books of humorous social commentary as well as
contributing to periodicals in England and America.

EVELYN WAUGH

MALCOLM BRADBURY

OLIVER AND BOYD
EDINBURGH AND LONDON

OLIVER AND BOYD LTD
Tweeddale Court
Edinburgh, 1

39A Welbeck Street
London W.1

First published 1964

Printed in Great Britain for Oliver and Boyd Ltd
by Robert MacLehose and Co. Ltd, Glasgow

CONTENTS

ACKNOWLEDGMENTS

I should like to express my gratitude to David Lodge, Bryan Wilson, Martin Green, and Bernard Bergonzi, all of whom either read this manuscript or discussed points about Waugh with me. Martin Green kindly let me see, and quote from, an as yet unpublished article. My wife gave me enormous help at all stages. For the provision of materials, I am most grateful to the Library of the University of Birmingham; and I owe a special debt to the East Riding County Library at Beverley, whose energies in obtaining rare books for me have been greatly appreciated.

For permission to quote from the works of Evelyn Waugh, acknowledgments are due to Messrs A. D. Peters, W. H. Allen & Company, Gerald Duckworth & Co. Ltd, and Little, Brown & Co.

Acknowledgments are also due to Chapman & Hall, Ltd (Frederick J. Stopp: *Evelyn Waugh: Portrait of an Artist*), and *Life* ("Fan-Fare").

The photograph on the front cover is reproduced by permission of Radio Times Hulton Picture Library.

M.B.

To
Bryan Wilson

ABBREVIATED TITLES BY WHICH THE WORKS OF EVELYN WAUGH AND OTHERS ARE CITED IN REFERENCES

B.M.	=	*Black Mischief.*
B.R.	=	*Brideshead Revisited.*
DeVitis	=	DeVitis, A. A.: *Roman Holiday: The Catholic Novels of Evelyn Waugh.*
D.F.	=	*Decline and Fall.*
E.C.	=	*Edmund Campion.*
H.	=	*Helena.*
H.D.	=	*A Handful of Dust.*
L.	=	*Labels: A Mediterranean Journal.*
L.O.	=	*The Loved One.*
M.A.	=	*Men at Arms.*
N.—T.D.	=	*Ninety-Two Days.*
O.G.	=	*Officers and Gentlemen.*
O.G.P.	=	*The Ordeal of Gilbert Pinfold.*
P.M.F.	=	*Put Out More Flags.*
R.	=	*Rossetti, His Life and Works.*
R.K.	=	*The Life of the Right Reverend Ronald Knox.*
R.L.	=	*Robbery Under Law.*
R.P.	=	*Remote People.*
S.	=	*Scoop.*
Stopp	=	Stopp, Frederick, J.: *Evelyn Waugh: Portrait of An Artist.*
U.S.	=	*Unconditional Surrender.*
V.B.	=	*Vile Bodies.*
W.A.	=	*Waugh in Abyssinia.*
W.G.G.	=	*When the Going was Good.*
W.S.	=	*Work Suspended.*

CHAPTER I

INTRODUCTION

Many intelligent readers of fiction find the novels of
Evelyn Waugh unattractive, regarding them as "pure
entertainment" or as "reactionary tracts." It is my
purpose here to suggest that Waugh is a remarkable
comic inventor, that his novels are modern both in
matter and manner, and that they add in a significant
and an original way to the stock of the English novel.
Waugh, however, has always been careful to avoid
making explicit statements that might support any reason
for taking him so seriously; offering himself as a stylist and
his work as an act of craftsmanship, he has implied that
those who go further do so at their own risk. He has,
indeed, carefully separated himself from his work; while
within the work itself one is conscious often that something is being reserved, that, as one critic has put it,
Waugh does not "press upon us the full complexities of
life."[1] To push further than this seems to be to enter a
world which, like the grounds of Waugh's country house,
is *interdite aux promeneurs*.

In recent years Waugh has presented himself as the
public private figure he drew for the electors when he
stood in 1951 as candidate for the Rectorship at Edinburgh
University:

I have never gone into public life. Most of the ills we
suffer are caused by people going into public life. I
have never voted in a parliamentary election. I believe
a man's chief civil duty consists in fighting for his King
when the men in public life have put the realm in

danger. That I have done. I have raised a family and paid such taxes as I find unavoidable. I have learned and practised a very difficult trade with some fair success. . . .[2]

Such statements depend upon pose and address; and Waugh is, of course, a modern version of that radical-reactionary the Dandy, whose history in the nineteenth century has recently been traced by Ellen Moers.[3] Beerbohm called the Dandy a man "with an oblique attitude toward life" and "a carefully cultivated temperament";[4] his first commitment was to taste and to aesthetic experience; he was inclined to see the aristocracy and a cosmopolitan viewpoint as a source of art; and in Decadent literature he was apt to unite a patrician stance with arts-and-crafts socialism in defiance of *bourgeois* and moralistic values. He was conscious of his pose—like Waugh's Mr Pinfold, who acts strenuously the part of "eccentric don and testy colonel" until it comes "to dominate his whole outward personality. . . . He offered the world a front of pomposity mitigated by indiscretion that was as hard, bright and antiquated as a cuirass."[5] The middle-aged artist of *The Ordeal of Gilbert Pinfold* (1957) is very much heir to Wilde and the Decadents; he is "fastidious," his "modesty" needs protection, and "for this purpose, but without design, he gradually assumed this character of burlesque." Artistically a writer of a silver age of letters, he ranks "quite high" among a literary generation "notable for elegance and variety of contrivance," but his work offers little to those who seek in it cosmic significance:

He regarded his books as objects which he had made, things quite external to himself to be used and judged by others. He thought them well-made, better than many reputed works of genius, but he was not vain of his accomplishment, still less of his reputation.

Unlike the great romantic artists, then, but like Wilde, Pinfold is not totally committed to his work, not given to an artistic dedication that promotes both his inspiration and his anguish. Pinfold's sense of the power and value of art is limited, and his stress falls on elegance of style, variety of contrivance, "professional trickery," and on art as self-concealment. In the social and religious realms also the Pinfold of this first chapter, a man committed to a style of life and pattern of taste opposed to those of most of his contemporaries, reserves his central modesty. The *ordeal* of Gilbert Pinfold is, however, a savage attack on that modesty by forces which appear to be outside but are really within himself. By the end of the novel he reasserts his old framework of reference but now, instead of its being a total understanding of the world, it is a battered fence against an anarchistic, antagonistic universe outside, a universe to which neither his religion, his aesthetics, nor his social values appear to have any positive answer. The world of reason totters back into control ... but control is not really exerted until Pinfold takes a new quire of foolscap and writes on it in "his neat, steady hand" *The Ordeal of Gilbert Pinfold*, the title of his new fiction—surely not a book "quite external to himself"?

The Ordeal of Gilbert Pinfold is the most revealing of all Waugh's novels, full of nuances that violate the popular view of him. A book about the dropping of a mask, the dandy's mask, it makes us wonder whether the mask has not been on and off for a long time. Further, it is a book about the incompleteness of the frame of reference we usually associate with him—and once again we wonder if this has not happened before. For Waugh has always been singularly protean, both as a social commentator and as a novelist. His open pronouncements have always been modulated through a comic self-presentation that reserves him from total involvement, while his fiction is likewise reserved because of the complexity and the indirection of his comic method and the peculiar amorality of his universe. There is in fact a permanent difficulty about picking up Waugh's tone; and to describe it and its implications is, for the critic who wishes to account for the effects and the effectiveness of his work, his most difficult single task. In the novels profound observation is thrown into question by a corroding irony; situations are established and then fail to yield up the expected interpretation; the pleasure Waugh takes in his characters is of a different order from his moral valuation of them. Many writers on Waugh have expressed a difficulty in discovering, within particular novels, a secure point of view; the intentions and values of the novelist have a way of appearing and then vanishing before their eyes. This is the repeated experience of those who have sought in the novels for a moral unity or secure system of values, because Waugh usually seeks his most powerful effects in another dimension. As one writer has put it, Waugh

> lures the reader into a judgment—in the context of neutral narration we are eager to accept one—and then leaves him there, the target of a hostility more supple and deep-seated than he had guessed.[6]

Another has observed that there is in the earlier novels "a very important element of perverse, unregenerate self-will that, giving rise to confusion and impudence, was a great asset for a comic writer."[7]

In fact, like Dickens's, Waugh's interpretation of situations is shaped to a large degree by the dramatic possibilities of the occasion and his own temperamental prejudices, so that a world can be without an apparent consistent point of view; like Dickens, he seems often to work by the scene or the chapter; like Dickens, one of the determining factors in his structure is a sense of comic possibility. His novels are, in this sense, anti-novels, violating traditional expectations, engaging extensively in mock-heroic or burlesque or parody passages, driven forward by a comic delight. Frequently there is an ironic uncertainty that works in another direction from the initial expectations aroused by the plot, and this indirection of development and obliqueness of treatment is intrinsic to his comic method, supporting the arbitrariness and variousness of his comic universe. His plots and tone depend heavily on his power to look sceptically at the novel as a *genre*, at himself as novelist, and at the values he is inclined to uphold. Often his social interests are superseded as another level of action dominates the book, reducing potential heroes to size and enlarging potentially anarchistic and harmful characters to a level of importance that, were he writing moral fables, they could not have if the pattern of the work were to be left intact. But, as in Byron's *Don Juan*, the framework he offers is usually supple enough to contain any form of action consonant with comic, anti-romantic, and occasionally romantic intentions.

This pattern is evident in all his work—the late as well as the early novels—in different forms. It provides it with its tension and its conflict, ultimately with its force. In the early novels the author offers an unredeemable and anarchistic universe with no secure centres of value and no real substantiation of any interpretative statements made in the course of the action. He works by "rendering," by offering us a universe from which he is largely detached, by using a Firbankian impressionism coupled with a precise social observation that gives the novels a contemporary reference yet exists within the framework of fantasy. He writes, unlike Firbank, without ostentation and without fuss; rather, his ostentation is entirely pointed in the direction of his complex comic effects and inventions. We admit the social truth of his observation, and *Vile Bodies*, for all its fantastic materials and its wholly invented World War, is truthful to the intellectual confusion and social gaiety of the nineteen-twenties.

There are firm points of authenticity that engage the reader in the meaning of the whole. As he develops, Waugh's methods gradually change. His prejudices, sympathies, social and religious values tend to be more actively engaged, but at the same time a compensating mechanism builds up the centres of opposition to them, so that those committed to his beliefs are shown as isolated, innocent and ripe for disaster. A larger part of the action than is technically necessary is devoted to characters who threaten or attack the centres of value. When the author's romanticism—for it is a romanticism of feeling that is released when the check of satirical or comic method is relaxed—is strongest, a countervailing principle points to its inadequacy or possible doom. In *A Handful of Dust*, Tony Last is treated sympathetically and his ambitions for Hetton are admired: but they are also shown to be incomplete, for the novel takes place in a universe of "nobody's fault." In other novels, *Put Out More Flags* and the unfinished *Work Suspended* for example, the author takes great pleasure in characters of whom he might be expected to disapprove in political or religious terms. Waugh's plots are set among a society in which possessions, the sense of cultural heritage and regard for certain sorts of social duty are common to the characters he seems to approve most; they are frequently about the pursuit of some human ambition, and turn on the failure of the pursuit. Both the aspiration and the failure are linked to an interpretation of history and a view of man which makes failure exceedingly likely. The universe in which the events occur is contingent and arbitrary. In its social aspects it is characteristically upper-middle-class or upper-class and often Catholic, but the events are chosen less to uphold or manifest values of either class or religion than to convey a comic world in which *all* values appear unreal. Thus, though the *milieu* of most of his novels is the silver fork world, the world of Society and the smart set, of an upper-middle-class and aristocratic coterie, usually metropolitan or with a metropolitan point of reference, it is also a fantastic universe. The traditional social comedy of manners of the kind sustained by Wilde or Ada Leverson is frequently converted into a fantastic comedy in which no values survive.

The debased and value-free world in which the comic action develops is an essential feature of Waugh's method. It is a world arbitrary, disorderly, meaningless— a "world of wild aberration without theological significance."[8] The characters who regard it as susceptible to order, coherence and control suffer for their innocence. They are usually treated sympathetically, and, as in the case of Tony Last, Guy Crouchback, or even Pinfold, they enshrine values towards which Waugh is deeply sympathetic. But they are mock-heroic figures on a mock-heroic quest. And repeatedly, in this same universe, Waugh shows the success of figures of whom he appears to disapprove, yet in whom he delights; Basil Seal, Margot Beste-Chetwynde and Ludovic are enjoyed by their inventor because of their comic possibilities and because they have the power to survive in such a world. Their successes are temporary, but their insolent anarchy is an important part of Waugh's romanticism. They are able to cope with the radical instability of the world-order to which Father Rothschild draws attention in *Vile Bodies*; Waugh clearly has a sense of some grim historical process working itself out (Lord Circumference, in *Decline and Fall*, asks Paul Pennyfeather if he thinks there will be another war—"Yes, I'm sure of it; aren't you?" says Paul; and the idea recurs from novel to novel). The view that we have passed into a special dark age is one that Waugh shares with many of the great novelists of the early part of the century. While his novels lack their human seriousness, they work in the same area of concern; and in the expansion of the comic and ironic method that has become distinctively the voice of twentieth-century scepticism Waugh's technical developments are significant. His feeling for the contemporaneous is an important aspect of his talent; he may look back romantically to an agrarian aristocratic past, but his present is distinctively modern, and he possesses the power to describe in a single stroke the flavour of a place, a mood or a person. He is the novelist of the culture of the gossip column and the motor race as well as of the country house. Further, he is in his approach to his materials urban and urbane, sceptical, often totally detached. His most powerful single effect lies in his invention of a comic universe seen from above by a creator largely independent of the action who, from a position of moral uninterest, perceives it as a total impression. His use of surrealistic techniques, his quick dialogue, his filmic technique of cutting rapidly from one locale to another, his manipulation of point of view, all tend to support his independence. His world is thus one of "prevailing carelessness," in which "the power, or will, to establish justice does not exist,"[9] and into which the characters mysteriously disappear, as does Paul Penny-feather in *Decline and Fall*. The comic tone thus becomes the means by which the moral expectations of the reader are absolved, and anarchy, roguery and sexuality become the norm. The traditional moral universe lies more or less outside the novel, to be recalled occasionally by a comment made by one of the characters, or by the introduction of a sudden feeling of tenderness and nostalgia which is Waugh's main means of reference to lost order.

Waugh's feeling is, then, that modern man is cut off from a common and mutually enlarging fund of values and institutions experienced in society at some time in the past; because of this recent fall, a man needs special powers to cope with modernity and the anarchy of a world internationalised, without values, lapsing into instability. Repeatedly in his novels he puts his characters to the test, to see how they encounter the special con-ditions of modernity. Frequently, as in *Vile Bodies*, the problem exists only for the new generation. Waugh's novels are usually written from the viewpoint of the age-group to which he belongs; the Bright Young Things become the Semi-Serious Middle-Aged Things and promise to become the Creaky Old Things. We live in an age of the rapid turnover of generations, and Waugh undoubtedly feels, as his father and brother did, that there is a radical difference between his generation and that of his parents. He is sentimental about the agrarian past from which we all, but especially the aristocracy, are exiled; houses, property and estates represent a kind of prelapsarian universe in which men were enlarged by institutions, moved in established grooves of conduct, and supported fine arts and craftsmanship. This world is, however, lost; a fall (the First World War?) has taken place and life has become a nightmare. In this situation the young are a suffering Elect who have the duty to violate the world of their parents. The older generation has "failed," largely through innocence, because they are incapable of perceiving the terms of the modern crisis. This view, slightly modified as Waugh himself grows older, is linked with his religious and social opinions, which gradually come to play a larger part in his fiction. In many of the novels these opinions are reserved—

The vision of barbarism is a farcical one, and the fantasy has its own vitality; the truth exists, self-evident, isolated from all this nonsense, and there is no need to arrange a direct confrontation—[10]

but in some of them, particularly in *Brideshead Revisited* and *Helena*, they enter the action; and in *The Ordeal of Gilbert Pinfold* and in the *Men at Arms* trilogy they are put to a test from which they do not emerge unscathed.

These religious and social opinions are well enough known. Waugh's conversion to Catholicism came early, when he was 26, and it was conversion to the entire reasonableness of the Catholic faith:

B

England was Catholic for nine hundred years, then Protestant for three hundred, then agnostic for a century. The Catholic structure still lies lightly buried beneath every phase of English life; history, topography, law, archeology, everywhere reveals Catholic origins. . . . It was self-evident to me that no heresy or schism could be right and the Church wrong. It was possible that all were wrong, that the whole Christian revelation was an imposture or a misconception. But if the Christian revelation was true, then the Church was the society founded by Christ and all other bodies were only good so far as they had salvaged something from the wrecks of the Great Schism and the Reformation. . . . It only remained to examine the historical and philosophic grounds for supposing the Christian revelation to be genuine. . . . [O]n firm intellectual conviction but with little emotion I was admitted into the Church.[11]

The intellectual and historical grounds of this conversion are of great significance for Waugh's work, for they involve the adoption of attitudes toward society and history that Waugh afterwards elaborated at length, and are most clearly to be seen in his travel books and journalism. The early travel-books are presented with the eye of a bright and brilliant young man who sees acutely but without system. Unlike Mr Pinfold, who abhors everything that has happened in his own lifetime, the young Waugh is curious about and takes great pleasure in the modern and the foreign—delighting in an aeroplane flight (*Labels*) and finding in Abyssinia a "crazy enchantment," a peculiar flavour of "galvanised and translated reality" (*Remote People*). Interested in absurdities and flavours, his curiosity is wide, so wide that he appends to the second edition of *Labels* (1932) a note saying that "my views on several subjects, and particularly on Roman Catholicism, have developed and changed in

many ways." Relishing "vitality and actuality,"
condemning "bogosity," he travels, as he tells us, with
"a mind as open as the English system of pseudo-
education allows,"[12] and manifests that education's main
product—a sense of period, the one common property of
every cultured Englishman. The main comparison
Waugh makes on his travels is between the civilisations,
cities and societies which manifest rich cultural and
artistic histories and styles of life, and those which are
arid, bogus or bare. His main standard of judgment is
aesthetic, with a strong social reference for his aestheticism; thus later in *Waugh in Abyssinia* (1936) he judges
Coptic ceremonial against European medieval church
culture—a culture "which had created an object of
delicate and individual beauty for every sensible use;
metal, stone, ivory and wood worked in a tradition of
craftsmanship which makes succeeding generations
complete [*sic*] for their humblest product";[13] and his
sympathetic presentation of Italian entry into the
country is offered largely on the grounds that an arid,
anarchic, uncultured society has been possessed by a
power prepared to make it into a working civilisation.
By this time, however, Waugh's philosophy has grown
more specific, radical in some of its implications but with
the idiosyncratic Toryism that is later attributed to
Pinfold. A sense of the failure of liberal humanism,
coupled with a sustained interest in it, runs through the
work of this period; a suspicion of the nonconformist
conscience, a distrust of all earthly régimes, a conviction
that things decline and fall as we move away from a total
Catholic *imperium*, a view of the world as a place where
the gates of the madhouse are periodically thrown open
(asylums and escaped madmen abound in his work) are
mixed with a patriotic ideal about his native land and
those who have nourished it and sustained its traditional
values. In *Robbery Under Law* (1939), Waugh enters the
politics he detests to show the futility of political action

and the way in which a nation wins by revolution only
the opportunity to try yet another kind of anarchy. He
finds Mexico a country without real conservers and this
causes him to state explicitly his Tory convictions—his
view that man is by nature an exile, that his chances of
improving his condition are small, that there is no form
of government ordained by God as being better than
any other, that men naturally arrange themselves into
systems of classes, that government is necessary because
of the anarchic impulse in mankind, and that Art is a
natural function of man which can exist in any social
system. In the book Waugh makes the analogy between
the present excess of political activity and the theological
activity that preceded church schism in the sixteenth
century, and remarks on the way in which "civilization,
like a leper" seems to be "beginning to rot at its
extremities."[14] His historical picture seems, in fact, to be
founded on the view that, by schism and political
activity, European Catholic civilisation went into a
decline which has gradually brought about a lapse into
anarchy, paganism and meaningless action. The honorific
words of the travel books are "justice," "charity,"
"reason," "traditional order," "ennobling institutions,"
and "fine workmanship." Political and economic
activity, having no super-ordinate values directing them,
are unserious, while their social influence and formative
power is played down. Traditional Catholic culture is
distinguished by its ideal of aesthetic fineness, by its
decency, order and good workmanship; these constitute
its special claims, and become the basis for Waugh's
highly ethnocentric conception of culture. In the
traditional Catholic civilisation the artist has a significant
role, interpreting the traditions and values of the culture
instead of commenting on it from outside—"The artist's
only service to the disintegrated society of today is to
create little independent systems of value of his own"[15]—
and living in a significant relationship with his universe

and his audience, one that survives into the patronage system. This civilisation is now declining; nonetheless it provides a basis for the pride Waugh experiences when he encounters cultures evidently defunct.

To Waugh, as Professor Kermode has pointed out,[16] the Church is a rational and sensible institution. Waugh comments approvingly of Ronald Knox's *Let Dons Delight* that it criticises "the factitious divorce of Reason from Revelation, leading to the denial of both."[17] The Church is, for Waugh, concerned with fact; it is a citadel of reason, clarity and beauty, but it must cope with what lies outside—anarchy, social decline, poor workmanship, and the uncreating word. Waugh's historical view of Catholicism means, of course, that it is necessarily identified with a failing social order; his rational view of it means that it is permanently threatened by anarchy. Indeed in a sense the anarchy has to triumph, for its persistence is the real basis for faith, a faith which thus becomes one of suffering and martyrdom. In this way Waugh's Catholicism is not big enough to contain the world; the spiritual life is separated from the real life, and two separate frameworks of experience are therefore possible, though the two can be reconciled by granting that God is purposeful in the world. It is this conflict, a conflict between the conduct of the spiritual life in an ideal realm, identified with a Golden City and a vanished civilisation in the past, and the conduct of diurnal life in the real world, that permits the existence of Waugh's comic universe. Moreover, since the assertion of his Catholicism depends on a pattern of stylish prejudice, delivered in the manner of Jowett's advice to the young— "Never apologize, never explain"[18]—and since it is not consistently maintained in the novels, it tends to seem less than a self-contained system of values. A new kind of martyrdom, the martyrdom of Pinfold, emerges. Pinfold does not lose his reason; indeed, in the state of hallucination from which he suffers "[t]he reason works with

enhanced power, while the materials for it to work on, presented by the senses, are delusions."[19] Waugh is capable of
questioning himself, not at the level of faith but at the level
of understanding. And it is in the power objectively to
pose this kind of challenge that he shows himself to have
his largest resources as a novelist. He is capable of an
extreme romanticism; his novels indeed *are* romances:
but the capacity for comedy and irony is what gives them
their real substance. The courtly hero, half Catholic, half
aristocratic, stands as a vague ideal figure behind some of
his later novels, but doubt, despair and anarchy are also
active in this universe. The sense of mission, the search
for the good, the pietistic subduing of self, have a positive
value for him, but it is of the failed search and the
uncompleted mission that he writes. He has a way of
emerging as a much more realistic and honest figure
than many of his more tendentious critics have allowed.

Certainly his novels do not create that sense of human
largeness and possibility we associate with the great
liberal strain in the English novel. He has few characters
to whom we feel very close or who represent striking,
endearing or responsible systems of value. In moments of
serious observation he tends toward the sentimental, the
nostalgic, the profoundly romantic. His aestheticism adds
further distance. His pleasure in the eccentric and
grotesque recalls Firbank as well as Dickens; his insistent
consciousness of novelty, of the new fashion and the smart
thing, recalls another late romantic, Scott Fitzgerald. He
belongs indeed to the tradition of the Gothic romance,
now turned to comedy. The conflict between the idealised
lost past and the need to answer to the present promotes
an elaborate comic structure—at best resolved entirely
on the comic level. One of the main lines of the development of the modern novel has been toward the extended
use of ironic comedy to convey the novelist's dialectical
tension and create a relationship with an audience on
whose values at any serious level he can place little

reliance. The liberal novelist disillusioned in his expectations of the future and the religious novelist confronting the spectacle of disintegrating faith are alike thrown back on personal systems of value and ironies of tone. Waugh solves the problem by writing at once social chronicle and fantasy in a spirit of comic delight that absolves him from consistent moral presentation. His comic power is, however, sufficiently rich and complex, sufficiently a consistent vision, to convey the "galvanized and translated reality" of the twentieth-century condition, and so to put him among the major comic novelists.

REFERENCES

1. Steven Marcus, "Evelyn Waugh and the Art of Entertainment," 1956, pp. 348 ff

2 Stopp, p. 45.

3. Ellen Moers, *The Dandy*, 1960.

4. Moers, *op. cit.*, p. 318.

5. *O.G.P.*, p. 9.

6. Graham Martin, "Novelists of Three Decades," 1961, pp. 394 ff.

7. Edmund Wilson, "Splendours and Miseries of Evelyn Waugh," 1951, pp. 298 ff.

8. *R.K.*, p. 314.

9. A. E. Dyson, "Evelyn Waugh and the Mysteriously Disappearing Hero," 1960, pp. 72 ff.

10. Frank Kermode, "Mr. Waugh's Cities," 1962, pp. 164 ff.

11. "Come Inside," 1949, pp. 10 ff.

12. *L.*, p. 16.

13. *W.A.*, p. 141.

14. *R.L.*, p. 3.

15. "Fan-Fare," 1946, 53 ff.

16. Frank Kermode, *op. cit.*, pp. 164 ff.

17. "Mgr. Ronald Knox," 1948, pp. 326 ff.

18. Edmund Wilson, "Never Apologize, Never Explain: The Art of Evelyn Waugh," p. 140 ff.

19. "Note," *O.G.P.* (American edn.).

CHAPTER II

PORTRAIT OF THE ARTIST

Evelyn Arthur St John Waugh was born on 28 Oct. 1903, of professional middle-class parents, in the London suburb of Hampstead. His father, Arthur Waugh, was a distinguished literary journalist of the eighteen-nineties, who had begun his literary career under the patronage of his distant cousin Edmund Gosse and was author of a life of Tennyson, one of the editors of the Nonesuch edition of Dickens, and from 1902 to 1929 managing director of the publishing firm of Chapman and Hall. He emerges from his pleasant autobiography *One Man's Road* as a typical member of that generation of men of letters, lively, critical, wide-ranging, close in spirit to the society of their time, who ran and wrote magazines in the late Victorian period. A self-confessed product of Victorian sentimentality, his tastes ran to his religion (Anglican), sport (particularly cricket), the countryside, and his old school (Sherborne) which he revisited regularly and to which he wished to send his two sons. His father was a Somerset doctor; his grandfather was Rector of Corsley, near Frome; his great-grandfather, who came from a family of bonnet-lairds, "farmer-proprietors, tilling the soil at East Gordon, a little village in Berwickshire,"[1] was a Secession church minister who became a distinguished London preacher. Arthur Waugh's wife, Evelyn's mother, was distantly related to the Cockburn family.

The family atmosphere seems to have been genial and lively, though Waugh has said that he never looked on his father other than as an old man, and that it was not until he was seven that he came to regard him as anything but an interloper.[2] Arthur Waugh recalls the young Evelyn, with his "precocious capacity for organising," marshalling a juvenile pistol-troop to defend England against Germans and Jews, declaiming at parties on behalf of female suffrage, manifesting religious interests. Evelyn Waugh has himself said that the enthusiasm his schoolfellows directed towards birds' eggs and trains he directed, at the age of ten, toward becoming a clergyman, and has spoken of his

strong hereditary predisposition toward the Established Church. My family tree burgeons on every twig with Anglican clergymen. My father was what was called a "sound churchman"; that is to say, he attended church regularly and led an exemplary life. He had no interest in theology. He had no interest in politics but always voted Tory, as his father and grandfather had done. In the same spirit he was punctilious in his religious duties.[3]

Waugh's older brother Alec went to Sherborne, where he was a somewhat rebellious pupil;[4] and before going into the army during the World War he wrote a *roman à clef* about the school, *The Loom of Youth*, published in 1917, which associated him with a general literary rebellion against the standards of his father's generation. The book overshadowed Evelyn's school career; it was thought advisable not to send him to Sherborne, for which he had been entered, and he was admitted instead to Lancing. Arthur Waugh saw the whole incident, together with the War, as "the end of our generation";[5] the way was paved for a new era of iconoclasts of which the Lancing prefect, bearing the "air of one who, as soon as he got to work in the world, would lose no time in putting down the mighty from their seat,"[6] was typical. Both young Waughs seem to have felt remote from their father's life ("Perhaps host and guest is really the happiest relation for father and son," Evelyn has written[7]), conscious of the total change in the flavour of life brought about by the War and aware of the loss of continuity that has made most people to-day "emotionally, displaced persons,"[8] while critics have noticed that Evelyn Waugh seldom depicts satisfactory relations between parents and children.

The choice of Lancing had a further significance: "We chose Lancing for Evelyn, when the barrier was set up against Sherborne, because he has always shown a deeply religious temperament, and we thought that the discipline of a Woodard School would be the best test of its sincerity."[9] Here a founder of the Dilettanti Society and the Corpse Club, he acquired a reputation as a flaunter of authority, a satirist and "a debunker."[10] He went on to read Modern History at Hertford College, Oxford, and felt himself "entitled to some self-indulgence."[11] "The decay of Oxford had barely begun,"[12] and Christopher Sykes finds in *Brideshead Revisited* "a truly successful description"[13] of the phase when traditional and ultra-modern values fused remarkably in a new aestheticism. The influential Harold Acton, with his taste for negro music, *chinoiserie*, French experimental writing and the music hall, began *The Oxford Broom* (to which Waugh contributed drawings and an early story) to sweep away "*fin-de-siècle* cobwebs." Acton describes the young Waugh in *Memoirs of an Aesthete* as a "faun half-tamed by the Middle Ages, who would hide himself for months in some suburban retreat, and then burst upon the town with capricious caperings."[14] Waugh mixed Conservative politics with radical literary associations, sharing the general feeling for dandyism and modernism.[15] He speaks of his Oxford life as unregretted but "idle, dissolute and extravagant."[16] After going down in 1924 without taking his degree he attended Heatherley's Art School "where I idled or played truant."[17] He became a schoolmaster at two private schools, being dismissed from one for drunkenness, and was for a short time a reporter on the *Daily Express*, nothing he wrote being printed. At this time "I was buying my clothes in Savile Row and Jermyn Street, running accounts at half a dozen shops and, when in funds, frequenting expensive restaurants."[18] Deciding to become a cabinet-maker in the country, he went during the autumn of 1926 to daily carpentry classes in Southampton Row. When he became engaged to the Hon. Evelyn Gardner, youngest daughter of Lord Burghclere, her mother found an engagement to a student carpenter preposterous and he "realised that there was nothing for it but to write books; an occupation which I regarded as both tame and exacting but in which I felt fairly confident of my skill."[19]

In 1926 his long story "The Balcony" appeared in *Georgian Stories*, edited by his brother Alec. Duckworth advanced him £50 for a book on Rossetti, published by them in 1928. *Rossetti: His Life and Work* draws on familiar scholarly materials, but the book expresses nicely Waugh's taste for the neo-Gothic,[20] his interest in Ruskin, Morris and the Pre-Raphaelites, and above all in the artist who unites literature and art. Waugh's approach is largely but not totally aesthetic; his Rossetti—

the baffled and very tragic figure of an artist born into an age devoid of artistic standards; a man of the South, sensual, indolent, and richly versatile, exiled in the narrow, scrambling, specialised life of a Northern City; a mystic without a creed; a Catholic without the discipline or consolation of the church—[21]

is criticised for his mediocrity, for lacking "the *moral* stability of a great artist,"[22] "that *essential rectitude* that underlies the serenity of all really great art. . . . There is a spiritual inadequacy, a sense of ill-organization about all that he did."[23]

In June 1928 the "secret wedding" that Acton describes in *Memoirs of an Aesthete* took place and the

Waughs went to live in Canonbury Square, Islington, where Waugh pursued "domestic arts and crafts" and appeared to have "a similar faith" to William Morris's.[24] The marriage was not successful, and broke up after a year, but his books were. *Decline and Fall* was taken as a satire on the nineteen-twenties and was much praised for its brilliance and maliciousness. It was found shocking by many, not least of all the publishing firm of Duckworth, to whom Waugh took the novel first; they rejected it "on what seemed, and still seems to me, the odd grounds of its indelicacy,"[25] requiring modifications to such details as Paul's running about without his trousers.[26] Waugh therefore took the novel to Chapman and Hall, the decision to publish being taken neither by Waugh's father or brother, but by R. E. Neale, who suggested a number of modest emendations—"He thought it, for instance, more chaste that the Llanabba Station Master should seek employment for his sister-in-law, rather than for his sister."[27] In 1930 Waugh's second novel *Vile Bodies* appeared, and was a popular success, largely because of its clear reference to the world of Mayfair and its parties, morals and Bright Young Things, in wild, mindless revolution against the preceding generation. It included such well-known figures as Aimée Semple Macpherson (Mrs Melrose Ape) and Rosa Lewis (Lottie Crump), and showed a world Waugh knew from within and rendered with considerable accuracy.[28] Readers found further interest in its feeling for the new things people could do—go to parties in dirigibles, fly in an aeroplane, make a talking film. Waugh confessed his taste for novelty in his next book, *Labels*, and saw a further use for it—"doing things which you think other people will find interesting" produced articles, got one's name into gossip-columns, and prevented the public from forgetting one's name "in between the times when they are reading one's books."[29]

Labels: A Mediterranean Journal (American title: *A*

Bachelor Abroad, A Mediterranean Journal), published in 1930—the product of the travels which Waugh (like his brother) embarked upon after his marriage collapsed— was the first of several travel-books he produced during the nineteen-thirties, his most prolific period. Waugh has described these books, written for money, as "pedestrian, day-to-day accounts of things seen and people met, interspersed with commonplace information and rather callow comments"[30] but they are more; he always has a sharp eye, a lively curiosity and a ready response to the absurd, and delights in evoking the anarchy of cities and societies, the difficulties of travel and the way in which it challenges or reinforces his temperamental prejudices. In *Labels* he is the bright young man, urbane, fond of comfort, fearful of "bogosity," curious about his situation, amused on religious matters. *Labels*, describing a Mediterranean journey on which his ostensible destination, Russia, is never reached, begins by speaking of "the hatred and weariness which the modern megalopolitan sometimes feels towards his own civilisation,"[31] divided between an allegiance to "sham modernity" and the sham past. So modern man is left with an aesthetic approach and an educated sense of period; and Waugh, detachedly wondering

how will this absurd little jumble of antagonising forces, of negro rhythm and psycho-analysis, of mechanical invention and decaying industry, of infinitely expanding means of communication and an infinitely receding substance of the communicable, of liberty and inertia, how will this ever cool down and crystallise out?[32]

concludes the book by speaking of the need to share a culture and a society in order to know "that whole cycle of rich experience which lies outside personal peculiarities and individual emotion"[33]—even though "everything one most loves in one's own country seems only to be the survival of an age one has not seen, and though all that one finds sympathetic and praiseworthy in one's own age seems barely represented at all in one's own country."[34]

On 29 Sep. 1930, Waugh, aged 26, was received into the Catholic church. After becoming an atheist at school he had begun "an unguided and half-comprehended study of metaphysics" which led him to believe that "man is incapable of knowing anything." Ten years of Mayfair life "sufficed to show me that life, there or anywhere, was unintelligible and unendurable without God"; foreign travel had revealed the "local, temporary character of the heresies and schisms and the universal, eternal character of the Church." Instruction by a Jesuit, Father Martin D'Arcy, brought intellectual conversion and life since has "been an endless delighted tour of discovery in the huge territory of which I was made free."[35] Immediately after his conversion he went as *Times* correspondent to Haile Selassie's coronation in Abyssinia and then visited Aden, Central East Africa and the Congo, reporting this in *Remote People* (American title: *They Were Still Dancing*) published in 1931. Well observed and witty, the book is concerned with the *Alice in Wonderland* quality of Abyssinia, its "crazy enchantment" deriving from the pretence of modernity imposed on an anarchic society. He examines the ceremonial of the Coptic church and finds it lacking the "clarity of the Western reason."[36] Critical of Westernisation in Africa, he reserves mild admiration for missionaries and the more rooted of Kenya settlers, for having transplanted and perpetuated "a habit of life traditional to them, which England has ceased to accommodate."[37] But the book ends with a nightmare scene in a London nightclub "hotter than Zanzibar, noisier than the market at Harar, more reckless of the decencies of hospitality than the taverns of Kabalo or Tabora,"[38] which ironically attacks Western civilisation.

The Abyssinian experiences appear, impressively

transposed, in Waugh's next novel, *Black Mischief* (1932).
Likewise a visit to British Guiana and the West Indies in
1932 yielded both a travel book, *Ninety-Two Days* (1934)
and some of the events of a fourth novel, *A Handful of
Dust* (1934). This journey arose from Waugh's interest in
"distant and barbarous places, and particularly in the
borderlands of conflicting cultures and states of development, where ideas, uprooted from their traditions,
become oddly changed in transplantation."[39] He characteristically plays down his own adventurousness, and
carefully debunks the glories of strange places and
people, of travel generally, and of travel-books. It is not
surprising that critics complained that travel seemed to
bore him. His next non-fiction book, a biography of the
Jesuit martyr *Edmund Campion* (1935), written to celebrate
the rebuilding in 1934 of Campion Hall, Oxford, is a
"simple, perfectly true story of heroism and holiness."[40]
Lucidly and finely written, the study emphasises that
Campion's mission was one without political motive, to
those who had the faith; and these were people of "the
most responsible and honourable class, guilty of no crime
except adherence to the traditional faith of their country,"
people whose choice lay between "the ordered, respectable life of their ancestors, and the faith which had
sanctified it" and who had chosen to follow holiness into
exile, imprisonment and death.[41] It is clearly Catholic
history, and Rose Macaulay is right to say[42] that the
account seriously underestimates the atmosphere of
conspiracy in Catholic quarters in the Elizabethan
period. Here begins Waugh's historical picture of an
England apostasising from Catholicism to schismatic
institutions leading to modern paganism;[43] he observes
that the Tudors left behind them a new aristocracy,
religion, and system of government which canalised the
vast exuberance of the Renaissance:

England was secure, independent, insular; the course

of her history lay plain ahead; competitive nationalism, competitive industrialism, competitive imperialism, the looms and coal mine and counting houses, the joint-stock companies and the cantonments; the power and weakness of great possessions.[44]

He bemoans the marginality of this new England, cutting itself off from the "great surge of vitality" arising from the Council of Trent—a marginality he is later to bemoan in present-day Catholicism, deprived of cathedrals and churches, ceremonial and fine liturgy—"Catholics meet in modern buildings, often of deplorable design, and are usually served by simple Irish missionaries."[45]

In late 1935 Waugh returned to Abyssinia to report the Italo-Abyssinian conflict for the *Daily Mail*—the only London paper that "seemed to be taking a realistic view of the situation," he said in *Waugh in Abyssinia* (1936), a book much criticised for its sympathy toward Italian action (a "Fascist tract," Rose Macaulay called it.[46]) Originally to have been called *The Disappointing War*, its aim is clearly to show that war is composed of aimless and desultory actions and cruelties and is quite unlike anything the newspapers, seeking news, and the politicians, supporting causes, claim it to be. Flippant, concerned with comic and aesthetic responses rather than with moral or political judgments, it praises the Italian occupation on the grounds that it brings to Abyssinia, in addition to some rubbish and mischief, "the inestimable gifts of fine workmanship and clear judgment—the two determining qualities of the human spirit, by which alone, under God man grows and flourishes."[47] This seems less than adequate in the situation, but it is less than adequate for Fascist sympathies either. Under his anarchy-seeking eye Abyssinia becomes "an archaic African despotism," "by any possible standard an inferior race" while imperialism, full of "avarice, treachery, hypocrisy and brutality" is seen as faintly better. The comic elements of his descrip-

tion, funny if cruel, reappear in fictional terms in *Scoop*
(1938), where one feels they belong. The disrepute into
which his attitude brought Waugh in intellectual circles
was reinforced by the stand he expressed on the Spanish
Civil War in a *Left Review* inquiry into writers' allegiances,
in which he said that if he were a Spaniard

> I should be fighting for General Franco. As an English-
> man I am not in the predicament of choosing between
> two evils. I am not a Fascist nor shall I become one
> unless it were the only alternative to Marxism. It is
> mischievous to suggest that such a choice is imminent.[48]

In 1936 Waugh's first marriage was annulled by a
decree of the Catholic church. In April 1937 he married
Laura Herbert, grand-daughter of the fourth Earl of
Carnarvon, and settled at Piers Court, Stinchcombe, a
sixteenth-century Gloucestershire manor, so becoming
the settled landowner of the later years. But his travels
were not over; with his wife he went, late in 1938, via the
United States to Mexico to see a dictatorship at first hand.
This was the régime of General Cardenas. The book that
emerged, *Robbery Under Law: The Mexican Object Lesson*
(American title; *Mexico: an Object Lesson*) is polemical
and, he tells us, political, "notes on anarchy." The
condition of Mexico—"waste land, part of a dead or, at
any rate, a dying planet"[49]—mirrors, for Waugh, that of
the world; but the absence of any genuine conservers
provokes him to express his own philosophy—that man
is, by nature, "an exile and will never be self-sufficient or
complete on this earth," that his chances of happiness
and virtue are little affected by the political and economic
circumstances in which he lives, that "sudden changes of
political condition are usually ill, and are advocated by
the wrong people for the wrong reasons":

> I believe in government; that men cannot live together
> without rules but that these should be kept at the bare

minimum of safety; that there is no form of government ordained from God as being better than any other; that the anarchic elements in society are so strong that it is a whole-time task to keep the peace. . . . I believe that Art is a natural function of man; it so happens that most of the greatest art has appeared under systems of political tyranny, but I do not think it has any connection with any particular system, least of all with representative government. . . .[50]

Though an attack on Cardenas's socialist régime for its expropriation of British oil interests and its persecution of Catholics, and by extension a critique of most militaristic and politically doctrinaire régimes (including Nazism), the book is chiefly concerned with the fear of anarchy. In this respect Mexico is a simple object-lesson:

Even at the time of writing when tempers are gloomier, the air is one of nervous vexation that progress should be checked by malicious intervention; progress is still regarded as normal, decay as abnormal. The history of Mexico runs clean against these assumptions. We see in it the story of a people whom no great external disaster has overwhelmed. Things have gone wrong with them, as they went right with us, as though by a natural process. There is no distress of theirs to which we might not be equally subject.[51]

Waugh holds that civilisation has no force of its own beyond what is given from within; it is under constant assault and takes most of the energies of civilised men to keep it going at all. Man is concerned not with progress but defence. "Barbarism is never finally defeated; given propitious circumstances, men and women who seem quite orderly, will commit every conceivable atrocity," and we are all "potential recruits for anarchy."[52] He appears to assume that men are not naturally and organically held in society; there is no God-given social order and the survival of law and government in any desirable form depends on a positive act of commitment. God would seem thus not to work in the world, and Catholicism becomes a theological, a-political philosophy; the separation of theology and politics that occurs in non-Catholic, liberal and militaristic societies thus enables his critique of politics. Since the main tradition of Catholic social thinking is much more organicist, Waugh's attitudes seem to be formed largely by his own personal observation of and reaction to modern society. *Robbery Under Law* depicts an anarchistic (sinful?) universe redeemed by the suppression of natural rebelliousness, and the book ends with what appears to be a penitential call to arms, which Waugh was shortly to answer with a new self—Waugh the warrior, the ideal soldier conserving, by fighting, the values of a civilisation that politics has brought into decay.

Perhaps Waugh's new spirit was to have been reflected in the evidently fresh manner of the novel he started just before the outbreak of War, but that event interrupted the book and it appeared as a fragment, *Work Suspended*, in 1942. Waugh became, instead, a soldier for English civilisation. He was commissioned in the Royal Marines in 1939, volunteered for the Commandos and served in the Middle East, then joined Brigadier Laycock's staff and transferred to the Horse Guards. In 1944, through the intervention of his friend Randolph Churchill, he joined Brigadier MacLean's Military Mission to the Yugoslav partisans. His literary production went on— *Put Out More Flags* (1942) was written on a troopship, and *Brideshead Revisited* (1945) after a parachuting accident when he was on indefinite leave of absence prior to the Normandy landings. He parachuted into Yugoslavia and according to *Life* magazine[53] the proofs of *Brideshead Revisited* were dropped to him there and corrected while he was hiding in a cave. He ended the War guilty about the decision to abandon the Allied landings in Yugoslavia, which involved leaving the country to Russian occupation and punishment.

Brideshead Revisited, though disliked by many critics, brought Waugh considerable fame and "unseasonable" success, selling nearly three-quarters of a million copies in the United States. It showed a religious concern new in his fiction and Waugh himself regarded it as a new departure:

> In youth I gadded about, and in those years and in the preposterous years of the Second World War I collected enough experience to last several lifetimes of novel writing. . . . When I gadded, among savages and people of fashion and politicians and crazy generals, it was because I enjoyed them. I have settled down now because I ceased to enjoy them and because I have found a much more abiding interest—the English language. . . . So in my future books there will be two things to make them unpopular: a preoccupation with style and the attempt to reproduce man more fully, which, to me, means only one thing, man in his relation to God.[54]

Waugh felt that the world he was settling down in was a darker one, as he showed when in 1946 excerpts from four of his pre-war travel-books were collected under the title *When the Going Was Good*:

> Those were the years when Mr. Peter Fleming went to the Gobi Desert, Mr. Graham Greene to the Libyan hinterland; Robert Byron . . . to the ruins of Persia. We turned our backs on civilisation. Had we known, we might have lingered with "Palinurus"; had we known that all that seeming-solid, patiently built, gorgeously ornamented structure of Western life was to melt overnight like an ice-castle, leaving only a puddle of mud; had we known man was even then leaving his post.[55]

Waugh did not cease travelling; a visit to Spain produced *Scott-King's Modern Europe*, a short novel (1947), and in 1947 a trip to Hollywood (to discuss and finally refuse a film offer for *Brideshead Revisited*) produced his one novel with an American setting, *The Loved One* (1948). In 1948–9 he went on two American lecture tours to Catholic institutions, including Loyola College, Baltimore, which in 1947 had awarded him an honorary degree, to speak on Ronald Knox, G. K. Chesterton and Graham Greene. He began to be regarded as a pillar of his society and his faith. In 1949 he edited a selection of Ronald Knox's sermons; in 1950 he published his religious-historical novel *Helena*; in 1952 there appeared, in a limited edition from the Queen Anne Press and with wood engravings by Reynolds Stone, *The Holy Places*, containing three items— an introduction called "Work Abandoned"; an essay originally devised for the B.B.C. in connexion with the dramatisation of the novel *Helena*, called "St Helena Empress"; and another essay, "The Defence of the Holy Places," an account of a visit paid to Jerusalem in 1951 under the patronage of *Life*, originally published in that magazine (24 Dec. 1951). In "Work Abandoned" Waugh tells of abandoning a project he had conceived at the age of thirty-two for a series of books, semi-historical, semi-poetic fiction, concerned with the intimate, intricate relations between England and the Holy Places, and dealing with such figures as Helena, Richard Lionheart, Stratford Canning and Gordon. Pride of country has, however, declined, England has surrendered "for low motives" her mandate to rule the Holy Land, Christian government and pious rebuilding there have ceased; and the series has been abandoned after *Helena*. The essay on the Holy Places, deeply serious in tone, details the history and present condition of the Church of the Holy Sepulchre, now a monument to the schism of the Catholic church, in disrepair and of uncertain future, yet still revealing the fire of faith:

One has been at the core of one's religion. It is all there, with all its human faults and superhuman triumphs, and one fully realizes, perhaps for the first time, that Christianity did not strike its first root at Rome or Canterbury or Geneva or Maynooth, but here in the Levant where everything is inextricably mixed and nothing is assimilated. . . . Our Lord was born into a fiercely divided civilization and so it has remained. But our hope must always be for unity, and as long as the Church of the Sepulchre remains a single building, however sub-divided, it forms a memorial to that essential hope.[56]

Waugh's dark view of Western civilisation remains, and so does his ethnocentric regard for the centrality of Catholicism, humanist, refreshed by "the great revitalizing power of the Counter-Reformation." Indeed his faith grows more explicit, more firmly insisted on. In 1952 appeared *Men at Arms*, the first of a trilogy of novels drawing on Waugh's military experience and using a specifically Catholic hero, Guy Crouchback. The second, *Officers and Gentlemen*, came in 1955, the third, after a long delay during which Waugh felt incapable of providing it, in 1961. The trilogy, battling against "the Modern Age in arms," was interrupted for the writing of three other books, all in a new more sober vein. *Love Among the Ruins* (1953) is a *jeu d'esprit* directed against the Festival of Britain, *The Ordeal of Gilbert Pinfold* (1957) an auto-biographical novel about an hallucinatory experience suffered by Waugh three years previous to publication. *The Life of the Right Reverend Ronald Knox, Fellow of Trinity College, Oxford, and Pronotary Apostolic to his Holiness Pope Pius XII* (1959) is a compilation from original sources, "the biography of a remarkable but rather low-spirited friend many years older than myself."[57] On Monsignor Knox's death in 1957 Waugh was left sole literary executor; he had previously written on Knox; and Knox, though knowing "my curiosity and lack of discretion,"[58] had already agreed to Waugh's plan to write his life. The book, discreet, sober, detailed, shows Knox's life as a tragedy of unfulfilment, almost as if his conversion from Anglicanism to Catholicism had taken him away from the main stream of his life. Waugh remarkably evokes the upper-middle-class culture, warm, assured, socially influential, from which Knox came and which he showed as writer and religious man. Though he finds Knox's comment on his conversion: "You'll be a more important person—but in a less important show" to be "contrary to all reason and observation,"[59] the book curiously supports the point.

The distance between earlier and later Waugh is evident in another travel-book, *A Tourist of Africa* (1960), written from the point of view of one who has seen another kind of life and looking over familiar territory in grumpy middle age:

> How gaily I used to jump into a taxi [in Paris] while the train crawled round the *ceinture*. Nowadays, hard of hearing and stiff in the joints, I sit glumly in my compartment.

Waugh the bright young thing and Waugh the warrior have in fact given way to Waugh the successful novelist and country gentleman, grumpy landowner at Piers Court and, more recently, at Combe Florey in Somerset. His fiction is widely known among an extensive circle of readers; most of his novels have appeared in a Uniform Edition and in 1951 Penguin Books issued paperback versions of ten of his works; he has just been elected a Companion of Literature. Like Pinfold he has stressed his privacy, like Pinfold he has "no ambition to lead or to command," like Pinfold he regards his faith as a totally personal matter:

> at the very time when the leaders of his Church were

exhorting their people to emerge from the catacombs into the forum, to make their influence felt in democratic politics and to regard worship as a corporate rather than a private act, Mr. Pinfold burrowed even deeper into the rock. . . . His strongest tastes were negative. He abhorred plastics, Picasso, sunbathing and jazz—everything in fact that had happened in his own lifetime. The tiny kindling of charity which came to him through his religion, sufficed only to temper his disgust and change it to boredom. There was a phrase in the 30's: "It is later than you think," which was designed to cause uneasiness. It was never later than Mr. Pinfold thought.[60]

Waugh's non-fictional writing shows the steady development of this figure of prejudice and pugnacity, the elderly dandy who lies behind the novels for which Waugh will survive. For though his biographical studies may remain interesting—and the biography of Knox has a clear scholarly value—and his travel-books, though ephemeral and demonstrating a vein of cultural prejudice that history is not likely to support, have their amusing and perceptive moments, the novels offer something more; within the aggressive landowner lies a remarkable literary imagination that puts his experiences, values and aesthetic ideas to complex uses. Indeed, his creative imagination, his comic inventiveness and responsiveness, is so strikingly different from his expressed opinions as to cause him to enter many dark places that Pinfold-Waugh seems likely to shun. Thus, though his writing deals with a small range of classes, quietly implies a Catholic frame of reference, and is frequently conceived in a vein of satiric cruelty that suggests extreme detachment, he has a comic inventiveness and an acute sensitivity to social flavour and to period which lead him into a deeper, richer level of experience set before us in a very different way.

REFERENCES

1. Arthur Waugh, *One Man's Road*, 1931, p. 60.
2. "My Father," 1962, pp. 4, 5.
3. "Come Inside." 1949, p. 12.
4. Cp. Alec Waugh, *The Early Years of Alec Waugh*, 1962.
5. Arthur Waugh, *op. cit.*, p. 364.
6. *Op. cit.*, p. 371.
7. "My Father," 1962.
8. Alec Waugh, *op. cit.*, p. 5.
9. Arthur Waugh, *op. cit.*, p. 367.
10. Dudley Carew, *The House Is Gone*, 1949, p. 93.
11. "My Father," 1962.
12. *Op. cit.*
13. Christopher Sykes, *Four Studies in Loyalty*, 1946, p. 80.
14. Harold Acton, *Memoirs of an Aesthete*, 1948, p. 126.
15. Cp. Acton, *op. cit.*; Alec Waugh, *op. cit.*
16. "My Father," 1962.
17. *Op. cit.*
18. *Op. cit.*
19. *Op. cit.*
20. Peter Green, "Du Côté de Chez Waugh," 1961, p. 90.
21. *R.*, pp. 13–14.
22. *R.*, p. 98.
23. *R.*, p. 227.
24. Acton, *op. cit.*, pp. 204–5.
25. "Introduction," *D.F.* (Revised edn.) 1962.
26. Alec Waugh, *op. cit.*, p. 203.
27. "Introduction," *D.F.* (Revised edn.) 1962.
28. Cp. Patrick Balfour, *Society Racket*, 1933; Acton, *op. cit.*; Alec Waugh, *op. cit.*
29. *L.*, p. 10.
30. *W.G.G.*, p. 9.
31. *L.*, pp. 14–15.
32. *L.*, p. 40.
33. *L.*, p. 206.
34. *L.*, p. 205.
35. "Come Inside," 1949, pp. 14–16.
36. *R.P.*, p. 89.
37. *R.P.*, p. 183.
38. *R.P.*, p. 240.
39. *N—T.D.*, p. 13.
40. *E.C.*, "Preface to the Second Edition," 1947.
41. *E.C.*, p. 114.
42. Rose Macaulay, "Evelyn Waugh," 1948, pp. 135–151.
43. Cp. Kermode, *op. cit.*, p. 166.
44. *E.C.*, p. 6.
45. "Come Inside," 1949, p. 13.
46. Macaulay, *op. cit.*, p. 146.
47. *W.A.*, p. 253.
48. Paul A. Doyle, "The Politics of Waugh," 1959, pp. 171–4, 221.
49. *R.L.*, p. 3.
50. *R.L.*, pp. 16–17.
51. *R.L.*, pp. 276–7.
52. *R.L.*, p. 279.
53. "Fan-Fare," 1946, p. 53.
54. *Loc. cit.*
55. *W.G.G.*, p. 10.
56. *Holy Places*, p. 37.
57. *A Tourist in Africa*, p. 13.
58. *R.K.*, p. 14.
59. *R.K.*, p. 176.
60. *O.G.P.*, pp. 3–8.

CHAPTER III

THE EARLIER NOVELS

Waugh's first work of fiction, *Decline and Fall: An Illustrated Novelette* (1928), is a picaresque comic novel describing the adventures of an innocent young man, a latter-day Candide, from the time when he is unjustly sent down from the Oxford college where he is reading for the Church, to the time a little more than a year later when he returns there disguised to resume his studies, having experienced in the meanwhile a world fantastic in its nature, totally challenging to all his assumptions. But if the picaresque form is characteristically that of a quest in which the hero is initiated into experience and acquires some truth—about his parentage, his values or the nature of mankind or society—which enables him to cope the better with his life, then Paul Pennyfeather's quest is a false one. Not only are the events he encounters fantastic and "unreal," "a lurid nightmare," but from them he learns that it is better not to learn, better not to try to cope with life, for it is a very strange affair indeed. The book involves an initiation, but of a strange sort; his most momentous discovery is that there are some people who should not immerse themselves too deeply in life's frenzy. Paul's values are extensively challenged and criticised, yet he returns to them, by now presumably conscious of their inadequacy. This is the only difference between the early Paul, bicycling "happily home from a meeting of the League of Nations Union" and the Paul of the last pages, who has "rejoined the League of Nations Union and the O.S.C.U." His liberal attitudes remain as they were; on religious matters he is (since he has been in a world of general licence) a trifle stricter: but he has returned to a world at odds with life as the middle part of the novel has shown it to him. His rebirth at the end is virtually a re-creation of his original self.

The social world of the novel, that of Waugh's own time, covers a wide variety of locales (London, Oxford, Wales, Marseilles, Corfu) and is centred largely on institutions and houses—Scone College, Llanabba School, King's Thursday, Blackstone Prison, Egdon Heath Penal Settlement and Cliff Place Sanatorium at Worthing—in all of which Paul finds a natural home and makes many casual and unexpected relationships over a wide social range. It is a world of chance relationships and passing encounters, of few beliefs and almost no duties, of sexual deviance and arbitrary death. This society is detailed largely at the upper-middle and upper-class levels, though what are usually known as "the lower orders" appear regularly and Dr Fagan confesses a marriage to one of them. The world of Mayfair, of which Waugh is considered to be a chronicler, appears only in the latter half of the novel. The book also involves two disparate systems of value, one associated with the genteel, *bourgeois* and Christian account of life, the other with the values of the fashionable smart set and with a pleasure-seeking and pagan attitude toward life, brought into contrast when Paul becomes involved with a rag initiated by the Bollinger Club, a traditional and exclusive Oxford society (treated by Waugh with interest but detachment). One of the Club thinks Paul's tie is the Club tie, worn under false pretences; he is stripped, and the following day sent down by the college for indecent behaviour.

The arbitrariness of this decision sets the tone for the whole book; this is a hard, unfair world, particularly but not only for those who have no right to wear the Bollinger tie. Paul is equally exploited by his solicitor-guardian and by Dr Fagan, the head of Llanabba School, who cheaply employs him. At the school Paul, essentially passive, adjusts rapidly and soon becomes popular in all quarters. His fellow masters—Captain Grimes, Mr Prendergast and Fagan himself—are all failed gentlemen, discards of an upper-class or upper-middle-class society, and the boys are much the same. Grimes's irrepressible exploitation of his social position—he is common but has an old school tie—and his constant ability to make his way in the world by getting others to put him on his feet ("It's out of the question to shoot an Old Harrovian") is a lesson for Paul, while Prendergast's doubts ("I couldn't understand why God had made the world at all") are something of a warning. But even Prendergast has his self-indulgence, and this is a world of self-indulgence, in which one can't, according to Grimes, "be unhappy for long provided one does just exactly what one wants to and when one wants to." It is the opposite of the world of ideals and asceticism that Paul left behind in his set at Scone, where people read papers on "Sex Repression and Religious Experience" and where his misfortunes are described as "injustice." When a friend from Scone, Stubbs, writes to Paul to tell him that he is refusing on Paul's behalf an offer from one of the Bollinger, Alistair Digby-Vane-Trumpington, "for sort of damages," Paul is forced to choose between the two worlds:

> "By refusing I can convince myself that, in spite of the unbelievable things that have been happening to me during the last ten days, I am still the same Paul Pennyfeather I have respected so long. It is a test-case for the durability of my ideals."[1]

He decides to refuse, explaining to Grimes that the money is rightly his, but there is the matter of honour:

> "For generations the British bourgeoisie have spoken of themselves as gentlemen, and by that they have meant,

among other things, a self-respecting scorn of irregular perquisites. It is the quality that distinguishes the gentleman from both the artist and the aristocrat. Now I am a gentleman. I can't help it: it's born in me. I just can't take that money."[2]

This class-contrast is emphasised throughout the book. But when Grimes sends for the money he feels "a great wave of satisfaction" and drinks a wry toast to "the durability of ideals"; his *bourgeois* standards are not so very durable, for they go against his inclination, against those "primitive promptings of humanity" Grimes is so in tune with. By several such comic events Paul's ideals are gradually rewritten for him, and he begins to move in the exotic world of the artist and the aristocrat, the bounder and the cad, where his liberalism is not disproved but simply becomes remote.

It is through one of these exotics, Margot Beste-Chetwynde, that Paul's situation alters and the book expands. Waugh treats her in a way that conveys less a justification of her conduct than a sustained interest in it. From her first appearance, when she arrives at the school "like the first breath of spring in the Champs Elysées,"[3] accompanied by Chokey, the exotic Firbankian negro, Waugh takes pleasure in her extravagance for its own sake. Margot is "a woman of vital importance," a cosmopolitan ("Are you in England for long?" she asks Lady Circumference, who replies "I live here") and a daring social deviant (hence Chokey). But she is also on the side of the natural, though it is a very stylised naturalness; and she rouses feelings of love in the passive Paul. But love can be dangerous, as we see when Grimes bemoans his approaching bigamous marriage to Flossie: "I'm one of the blind alleys off the main road of procreation, but it doesn't matter. Nature always wins. . . ."[4] Grimes saves the day, after the marriage has taken place, with a faked suicide, decked out with a message of warning for natural man: "THOSE THAT LIVE BY THE FLESH SHALL PERISH BY THE FLESH."

On this note the first part of the novel closes, and the second opens with a change of setting, pace and point of view. Paul has now been engaged by Margot as tutor for her son, Peter, one of Paul's Llanabba pupils, and the action is transferred to the metropolitan social scene, where Waugh's interest in the doings of the smart set becomes pronounced. The opening chapter of this second part, a chapter from which Paul is entirely absent, sets the tone of this world, for it tells of Margot's purchase and rebuilding in the modern manner of King's Thursday, the historic Hampshire seat of the Pastmasters. It is interesting that Waugh does not treat the Pastmasters' selling of the house unsympathetically, as some critics have suggested; his amusement turns rather against the antiquarian clergymen and Jack Spire of the *London Hercules* who start a Save King's Thursday Fund. The rebuilding, by Professor Silenus, the modernist architect, is offered symbolically; Margot finds Tudor architecture "bourgeois" while Silenus sees the problem of modern architecture and art as "the elimination of the human element from the consideration of form" because all evil comes from man:

What an immature, self-destructive, antiquated mischief is man! How obscure and gross his prancing and chattering on his little stage of evolution! How loathsome and beyond words boring all the thoughts and self-approval of this biological by-product! this half-formed, ill-conditioned body! this erratic, maladjusted mechanism of his soul: on the one side the harmonious instincts and balanced responses of the animal, on the other the inflexible purpose of the engine, and between them man, equally alien from the *being* of Nature and the *doing* of the machine, the vile *becoming*!"[5]

Paul encounters the curiously linked worlds of naturalism

and mechanism when he goes to King's Thursday, set in "the dreaming ancestral beauty of the English country," its great chestnuts seeming to stand for "something enduring and serene in a world that had lost its reason and would so stand when the chaos and confusion were forgotten":

And surely it was the spirit of William Morris that whispered to him in Margot Beste-Chetwynde's motor car about seed-time and harvest, the superb succession of the seasons, the harmonious interdependence of rich and poor, of dignity, innocence, and tradition?[6]

But from this he goes straight into the futurist world of the house, vulcanite, aluminium and black glass, with its "sleepless, involved genius." Set in nature, it manifests rather the contrived, anguished elegance of Margot, who now appears "from her little bout of veronal, fresh and exquisite as a seventeenth-century lyric." Margot wants to marry Silenus, yet picks out the unlikely Paul to spend a very modern night of love with her. In love and still totally innocent, Paul undertakes a commission for Margot, whose "business"—involving the resurrected Grimes and the ubiquitous school butler Philbrick –is white slaving. The comedy here is that of experience looking with a laughing eye on Innocence; Margot's corruption is made evident in passages treated with complete ethical neutrality. Paul is to marry Margot but is arrested on his wedding day and saddled with full responsibility for her activities. Imprisoned, he adjusts to yet another change of fortune with the usual passivity and equanimity, enjoying the freedom from responsibility:

It was so exhilarating, he found, never to have to make any decision on any subject, to be wholly relieved from the smallest consideration of time, meals or clothes, to have no anxiety whatever about the kind of impression he was making; in fact, to be free.[7]

Paul's great moment of freedom is however incomplete, since he has to solve the problem of his moral response to Margot; and here he finds himself torn between two conflicting forms of thought, between a traditional and a modern view of her behaviour:

> On one side was the dead weight of precept, inherited from generations of schoolmasters and divines. According to these, the problem was difficult but not insoluble. He had "done the right thing" in shielding the woman; so much was clear, but Margot had not quite filled the place assigned to her, for in this case she was grossly culpable, and he was shielding her, not from misfortune or injustice, but from the consequences of her crimes. . . . As he sat over his post-bags he had wrestled with this argument without achieving any satisfactory result except a growing conviction that there was something radically inapplicable about this whole code of ready-made honour that is the still small voice, trained to command, of the Englishman the world over.[8]

Paul is finally convinced that there is "one law for her and another for himself, and that the raw little exertions of nineteenth-century Radicals were essentially base and trivial and misdirected," recognising that Margot is a creature of a different, evolving species lying outside conventional moral expectations and laws. The point is reinforced when Grimes appears in prison and, unlike Paul, refuses to accept it, quickly making his escape by feigning another death. He is not, like Prendergast and Paul, mortal, but is "one of the immortals. He was a life force." The world of the life-force is the world of the comic and the amoral and the lawless, and Paul is being put to the test of whether he can enter the comic universe, which in Waugh becomes an ethic demanding appreciation for its own sake—an appreciation few Waugh heroes give totally.

The moment of test is the turning point of the novel; it comes when Paul too escapes from prison, through arrangements made by Margot and winked at by the authorities, and his death too is pretended—a death in which, as Dr Fagan (now transmogrified into the proprietor of the Worthing sanitorium where the "demise" takes place) says, all the characters are participants. Now Paul can be whatever he wishes. His progress has been toward an amoral system of life in which there exists an elite of the natural, the untrapped, the self-defined, the phoenixes who, like Grimes, can move unseen when darkness covers the waters. These natural Pan-like figures—comic versions of those which populate the novels of Forster and other contemporaries —represent a style of life belonging to a world without law, where desire runs free—Grimes surely "taught the childish satyrs the art of love." Paul goes to Corfu to choose himself, and meets Professor Silenus, who has just come from Greece, disliking the buildings but liking the goats. (The wise Silenus, companion to Dionysus, is Nietzsche's satyr-god of comedy who leads the "chorus of natural beings who as it were live ineradicably behind every civilization" and celebrate in art the Dionysian frenzy, "a complete sexual promiscuity overriding every form of established tribal law.") Silenus compares life to the Big Wheel at Luna Park, where, in the centre of a room with tiers of seats all round, the floor slowly rotates and people try to sit on the wheel and are flung off— "and that makes them laugh, and you laugh too." Someone stands in the centre, often "paid by the management," and sometimes does a sort of dance.

Of course at the very centre there's a point completely at rest, if one could only find it: I'm not sure I am not very near that point myself. Of course the professional men get in the way. Lots of people just enjoy scrambling on and being whisked off and scrambling on again. . . .

D

Then there are others, like Margot, who sit as far out as they can and hold on for dear life and enjoy it. But the whole point about the wheel is that you needn't get on it at all, if you don't want to.[9]

People think they have to join the game even if they don't enjoy it; and Silenus tells Paul he is a person who clearly should stay in the seats and watch, though somehow he is on the wheel:

It's all right for Margot, who can cling on, and for me, at the centre, but you're static. Instead of this absurd division of people into sexes they ought to class people as static and dynamic.[10]

So Paul chooses to become his old self again, accepting Silenus's distinction. He returns in disguise to Oxford to take up the life in which he was interrupted, picking similar friends among gauche young liberals (Stubbs instead of Potts) and manifesting strict views on heresy, particularly where it has to do with freedom of the natural urges. The novel closes when he meets again his favourite pupil Peter Beste-Chetwynde, Margot's son, now a Bollinger member, and learns that she has not only married Lord Metroland but has Alistair Digby-Vane-Trumpington for a lover. Paul tells Peter that he remembers the whole interlude but must forego all it meant to him. "We're different somehow," Peter tells him, and Paul says, "I know exactly what you mean. You're dynamic, and I'm static." On this separation the novel ends.

Of course this action is "fantastic,"[11] highly stylised, suited only to a comic novel. Yet it is an archetypal, masterful comic plot. The way in which characters return again and again in different roles or guises (as Partridge does in *Tom Jones*) is part of the novel's burlesque quality, demanding that we accept a different set of probabilities than those in life. Paul, a traditional comic hero, is used in two ways, as the comic agent whose movement through a varied world creates a line of action, and as the victim of a set of comic misfortunes which he constantly suffers yet constantly escapes—so ending the book, after repeated deprivations of all he owns or values, in the situation with which he began. From the start we know that this is a world which is arbitrary, without anything but the *appearance* of justice, the moral and legal codes being exploited for the convenience of the characters; but a comic, other justice works itself out. The probabilities are that those who have the chance to profit from others' misfortunes will do so, that those who have ideals will suffer for them, that honour will not serve one well. The social probabilities are just as free; here one may meet anyone and anything can happen. Our attention is drawn to the amount of coincidence—"Rather a coincidence, isn't it?" remarks the ubiquitous Grimes when he turns up again in prison with Paul; and Dr Fagan, whose fortunes are strange and various but coincide often with Paul's, puts the point more stylishly when he declares the participation of most of the characters in Paul's mock death:

"When you get to my age, if you have been at all observant of the people you have met and the accidents which have happened to you, you cannot help being struck with an amazing cohesiveness of events. How promiscuously we who are here this evening have been thrown together! How enduring and endearing the memories that from now onwards will unite us! I think we should drink a toast—to Fortune, a much-maligned lady."[12]

This toast, drunk recurrently throughout the novel, emphasises the way in which, in the arbitrary Waugh universe, accidents, chance, strokes of fortune or misfortune are at the heart of his plots. We must accept as probable the sending down of a man for no other reason than that he has been the victim of a rag, and we do, because of the kind of relation with reality the book creates. Paul's being sent down is painful only in a novel-world in which success in one's chosen career is important; likewise his being in prison will be tragic only if he is madly in love with Margot, feels profoundly cheated by her, or positively values freedom. In fact his feelings for Margot are as lightly sketched as is the activity of his moral life. Characters, drawn largely for their comic traits, never exist in any complex interrelation with one another; their emotions are lightly defined, their psychological life is only touched on, they do not develop in any deep sense. The area in which they can suffer is so controlled that misfortune is never important; it takes on a comic face. When a "serious" incident does take place, like the killing of Prendergast, the manner of presentation is sufficient to relieve concern. Paul enters a world where justice, fairness, kindness are forgotten—though for the comedy to work these things must never be forgotten by the reader. It is certainly a careless and cruel universe, containing a careless humanity, a universe in which, in A. E. Dyson's words "the power, or will, to establish justice does not exist," and in which compassion is deliberately withheld:

> At the end, [Paul's] supposed death, narrated with mock-heroic echoes of Tennyson's *Morte d'Arthur*, is at the level of satire a comment on the final stage of his disappearance. His "resurrection" is an ironic bow to the resilience of such shades in the waste land, and in no sense a re-establishment of concern.[13]

Certainly this is that kind of comedy that Bergson describes in *Le Rire*, an activity of the intelligence only— "the comic demands something like a momentary anaesthesia of the heart." The opinions and judgments we have about the hero—a modest degree of sympathy and affection, induced and yet modified by the very largeness of the misfortunes he undergoes, and his "shadow" state—are carefully managed to this end.

The most revealing indication of the comic method occurs in the second chapter of part two where Waugh, hitherto the detached narrator, intervenes to explain the relationship between novelist and hero and so establishes firmly (as do Fielding's interventions in *Tom Jones*) the unreality of the invented world of comic myth. For a moment we see "the Paul Pennyfeather who had been developing in the placid years which preceded this story," and Waugh says:

> the whole of this book is really an account of the mysterious disappearance of Paul Pennyfeather, so that readers must not complain if the shadow which took his name does not amply fill the important part of hero for which he was originally cast.[14]

By contrasting the world beyond and that within the story, Waugh makes clear the special expectations of a comic universe, in which Paul must be an anti-hero in an anti-novel, his only importance arising "from the unusual series of events of which his shadow was witness."[15] He leaves life and enters the world of comic universals, improbable but consistent within itself, for the characters act by devised rule. Fiction is stylised discourse as well as representation of life, and though, as the title's reference to Gibbon suggests, Waugh is concerned with the follies of the nineteen-twenties, he approaches them obliquely, with comic abstraction. Thus he satirises the radical and the reactionary alike (the two prison governors), and delights both in Paul and the larger, amoral universe with which he cannot cope. The book is indeed a comic ritual of Innocence, in which an uninitiated simpleton encounters the wickedness of the adult world, becomes involved in situations of guilt resulting in unearned punishment, and is restored to primary Innocence by his counterfeit death.[16] But each world is reduced to size by the other; there is comedy at the expense of innocence and satire at the expense of experience.

In Waugh's second novel, *Vile Bodies* (1930), he approaches his materials and forms his world in rather a different way. This is a comedy of manners with a strong element of fantasy and surrealism. There are no two worlds of action, nothing within the book to denote reality, no hero who is outside the values of most of the characters of the novel and is thus critic and victim of its events. All the characters and locales are totally involved in the world of frenetic gaiety the book creates, the world of the urban smart set in the late nineteen-twenties. In *Decline and Fall* this world of the Bright Young Things is seen from the point of view of the outsider, Paul, to whom it represents a moral challenge; in *Vile Bodies* the hero, more lightly defined, is of the set, while the set comes to the centre of the novel and is impressionistically offered to us in detail and breadth. A number of characters from *Decline and Fall* reappear—Margot Metroland, the Hon. Miles Malpractice, Peter Pastmaster, Alistair Digby-Vane-Trumpington, Lady Circumference—but they are represented as characteristic of a generation in rebellion against traditional moral codes. Their rebellion is, however, "not experimental, but fashionable," a "revolution in manners stabilized, popularized, flattened out."[17] The social life of the book is drawn from the upper class and upper-middle class of the English nineteen-twenties in its urban and cosmopolitan Mayfair circumstance, at a time when, according to Patrick Balfour,[18] the aristocracy of birth was replaced by one of wealth, cosmopolitan, with a feeling of alienation and anonymity, a strong herd-sense, a fondness for the sensational, a new and instinctive morality, an uncertain income and an awareness that the world was no longer personal but impersonal. The action happens largely among the younger generation, who bear the brunt of the new tension and are shown as intrinsically different from their parents; they

are conscious of themselves as a generation, a feeling
facilitated by female emancipation; their life is made up
of travel, parties, sexual and other deviance, and the
dedicated pursuit of fun, outrageousness and novelty.
The divided generations form the two sectors of value,
separated in understanding and purpose. The Bright
Young Things resemble the herd in *The Sun Also Rises* in
forming an exclusive elect, allowing entry only to those
who are modern in the right, the group-approved, way,
dividing the world into the "amusing" and the "bogus"
and regarding those not of their class or style—like Miss
Mouse, the American judge, and the older generation
generally—as outsiders, colourless and out of touch.
They are contained within a wider society (whose social
range includes deposed Ruritanian royalty and two
alternating Prime Ministers) to the social and political
processes of which, decisive as these prove, they pay little
attention. A reason for their conduct is offered by Father
Rothschild at the party at Anchorage House, where the
older generation meets and the "topic of the Younger
Generation spread through the company like a yawn."
The Prime Minister complains that there is a whole
civilisation to be saved and re-made, and the young only
play the fool. Father Rothschild speaks of a forthcoming
war ("there is a radical instability in our whole world
order . . .") and suggests that people don't want to lose
their faith:

> "I know very few young people, but it seems to me
> that they are all possessed with an almost fatal hunger
> for permanence. I think all these divorces show that.
> People aren't content just to muddle along nowa-
> days. . . ."[19]

The remark is comically obscure and not totally authoritative, but it certainly indicates why the world of
Anchorage House is not the centre of positive value in the
novel, why there is a necessary alienation from it. The

older generation is out of touch with the tensions of the times, and even the "great concourse of pious and honourable people" that Waugh celebrates is identified with the dull, docile and out-of-touch. The novel begins with all the main characters suffering together on a bad cross-Channel crossing, "unhappy about the weather" ("to avert the terrors of sea-sickness they indulged in every kind of civilized witchcraft, but they were lacking in faith") and ends with a fantastic World War between undefined powers which provides *post facto* support for Father Rothschild's "radical instability." Though offered salvation in various forms, from the social religion of Father Rothschild, the rich priest with "penetrating acumen" and access to all the councils of the great, to the evangelism of Mrs Melrose Ape and her rather battered group of Angels, the Bright Young Things seek it in fun. They are nearer to Doubting Hall than to Anchorage House. When they are "parched with modernity" they can go to Shepheard's Hotel in Dover Street and "draw up, cool and uncontaminated, great, healing draughts from the well of Edwardian certainty": but their taste is for the "faster, faster" of Agatha Runcible, for they belong to a civilisation running off the rails. The vague reference to war in *Decline and Fall* quietly dominates *Vile Bodies*.

It is not until the second chapter that Adam Fenwick-Symes, a novelist about whose appearance there is "nothing particularly remarkable" is selected as hero. He is not as independent of the world in which he finds himself as Paul, but he has reservations about it:

"Adam, darling, what's the matter?"
"I don't know. . . . Nina, do you ever feel that things simply can't go on much longer?"
"What d' you mean by things—us or everything?"
"Everything."
"No—I wish I did. . . ."[20]

This is lightly sketched, but it is essential to his role, both as a spokesman of the Bright Young Things and as a mild critic of them. Adam lies half-way between the Innocent hero (Paul Pennyfeather) and the Bounder hero (Basil Seal). At the beginning of the novel he is deprived and made innocent when a customs officer confiscates and burns his new book—significantly an autobiography—with which he was to finance his marriage to Nina, to whom "in the course of his correspondence" he has become engaged. But he has the sophistication of his *milieu*, and at the end of the book triumphs caddishly over the innocent Ginger, who has married Nina after Adam has sold her to him to pay off his debts, by impersonating Ginger and appearing as Nina's husband at Doubting Hall. The plot of the novel is about money, the need to possess it and the ease with which it is won or lost. Though essential, absolutely a condition of marriage, it comes from casual sources and symbolises a spendthrift attitude in society towards its security. Adam borrows, gambles, even takes a job (to do it quite unseriously) and much of the action is concerned with a chase for a lost thirty-five thousand pounds, the winning of a possible bet placed by an unknown major on Adam's behalf. On this sum Adam's marriage to Nina depends; finally, broke, he sells her to Ginger, then triumphs in a mock-marriage rather like Paul's mock-death. The other main line of development is the steadily hastening round of parties—"(. . . Masked parties, Savage parties, Victorian parties. . . dull dances in London and comic dances in Scotland and disgusting dances in Paris—all that succession and repetition of massed humanity. . . . Those vile bodies. . .)"[21]— culminating in the mad motor races that lead to Agatha Runcible's death. But throughout the casualties are heavy; and Adam's role as hero is related to his capacity to survive.

The main comic effect is once again that of deprivation

of hopes and possessions in a world without value or meaning. Values exist in the past, where "certainty," "permanence," "honourable people," and "faith" are vaguely located, but they exist (like most established attitudes in the early Waugh) to be violated. *Vile Bodies* is perhaps the most metropolitan and detached book of a cosmopolitan novelist, concerned about but also manifesting the terrifying and sophisticated brightness of the nineteen-twenties. Waugh's sympathies are imprecise; his presentation of the desultory undemanding relationship, the casual sexual encounter, the marriage based only on a taste for sensation is flat and impressionistic; his pleasure is in flavour and incident and character, and most explicit statements must be taken as helping along the action rather than conveying his attitudes. He has been called "the Pillar of Anchorage House" but in fact he emerges closest to the young; the old, who criticise them, are not outside the farcical universe, and though in some passages, like the description of Christmas at Doubting Hall, Waugh is clearly engaged, his main purpose is contrast. Certainly the meaning of the novel's events can only be explained in terms of a social, political and religious decline, but Waugh's main focus is on their comic potentiality. There is no real analysis of the political situation, though a political process works itself out "behind" the book to culminate—in the "Happy Ending"—with the biggest battlefield in the history of the world. Waugh certainly discerns an historical cause which makes people behave more wildly, run faster, foresake traditional values, fight wars, but his first interest is in depicting those things through a technique of comic fantasy not unlike that of *Through the Looking Glass*, to which he alludes several times. Growing frenzy, sudden death, mad chases develop surrealistically in the novel, so that fantasy comes to dominate over the satirical intentions. His use of heightened unreal situations, drawing on techniques of *grotesquerie* found in

Dickens and Firbank and also in his surrealistic contemporaries, produces a total departure from reality. The directly rendered impressionistic effects, the use of filmic cutting, the absence of reflexion and ratiocination either by author or agents, the preponderance of dialogue, the wealth of characters, the light definition given to them (down to the use of Restoration comedy or Dickensian names), their use in scenes of crowd burlesque, all this throws the emphasis on the comic aspects of the work, the author's power of fantastic invention. The novel is concerned with the decline of the West, but large parts (Agatha at the races, Adam as Mr Chatterbox, the seduction at Arundel) are devoted to a "joyfully insolent defiance of reason and right,"[22] and the riotous anarchy of comedy dominates the novel.

Black Mischief (1932) shows an interesting difference in its mixture of realism and fantasy; the fantasy aspects occur particularly in the imaginary kingdom of Azania (frankly drawn from Waugh's visit to Abyssinia and Zanzibar) while the London scenes are treated with a new realism. The social life of Mayfair, though it occurs in roughly the same group (several characters recur from earlier novels, including Alistair Trumpington and Peter Pastmaster), is presented in a less heightened, more detailed way that emphasises the sour and sordid aspects of this life; the "rackets" are more menacing and violent, while the realistic detail in which Angela Lyne and Lady Seal are drawn as characters makes Basil Seal's exploitation of them much more criminal. During the course of the novel many of the Bright Young Things "get very poor"—"Everyone's got very poor and it's made them duller"[23]—and the increased seriousness of the set at the end is given great significance. Seal is also a new kind of hero, one of the novel's *two* heroes. His drunkenness, pugnacity and "rackets" are more than bids for attention; they are manifestations of deep-seated discontent and excused in those terms:

He stood in the doorway, a glass of whiskey in one hand, looking insolently round the room, his head back, chin forward, shoulders rounded, dark hair over his forehead, contemptuous grey eyes over grey pouches, a proud rather childish mouth, a scar on one cheek.

"My word he is a corker," remarked one of the girls.[24]

Agressively the Bounder, he lies somewhere between the reprobate gentleman hero (Raffles, Clovis, Bulldog Drummond) of the early part of the century and the lower-middle-class rebel hero of the nineteen-fifties. His irresponsibility is described in terms of rebellion; he moves away from duties and from definition and it is only when, tired of London, he goes to Azania that he finds a use for himself. In his whole manner and range of vices he expresses the general insolence and amorality that Waugh has spread widely over his earlier novels. In the island kingdom of Azania, off Africa, he encounters the Emperor Seth, Chief of Chiefs of the Sakuyu, Lord of Wanda and Tyrant of the seas, Bachelor of the Arts of Oxford University, and the second hero of the book. Waugh seems to desire to combine his sense of an anarchistic universe with the presentation of the tragic situation of those who are involved in trying to bring order to it. He moves here toward tragic farce; and achieves it by contrasting a hero who has the natural power of a Grimes to survive with another who is necessarily a victim. For Seth believes in Progress:

"I have been to Europe. . . . I have read modern books —Shaw, Arlen, Priestley . . . at my stirrups run woman's suffrage, vaccination, and vivisection. I am the New Age. I am the Future."[25]

and unlike his predecessor, who plays the Waugh game, he is trying to bring it about through conviction and not for political advantage. Seth is one of Waugh's innocent

heroes, farcical because of the *mélange* of more or less
self-contradictory progressive reforms he conceives, based
on "a confused sediment of phrase and theory, scraps of
learning half understood and fantastically translated,"
serious because of his fate and the difficulty of his
situation, suspended between "civilisation" and barbarism:

> Night was alive with beasts and devils and the spirits
> of dead enemies; before its power Seth's ancestors had
> receded, slid away from its attack, abandoning in
> retreat all the baggage of Individuality; they had lain
> six or seven in a hut; between them and night only a
> wall of mud and a ceiling of thatched grass; warm,
> naked bodies breathing in the darkness an arm's reach
> apart, indivisibly unified so that they ceased to be six
> or seven scared blacks and became one person of more
> than human stature, less vulnerable to the peril that
> walked near them.[26]

Here is a tension more deeply defined than anything in
the earlier novels, and there is a new purposefulness in
the fact that Seth suffers and Basil to some degree learns
("I think I've had enough of barbarism for a bit," he
says at the end; and Sonia Trumpington remarks,
"D'you know, deep down in my heart I've got a tiny
fear that Basil is going to turn serious on us too"). The
contrast between Basil, "insolent, sulky, and curiously
childish," given to mischief, temperamental action, caste
snobbery, and Seth, dedicated to a progress whose
sterility is shown by the Birth Control campaign, turns
on the fact that one of them reacts against culture, the
other against anarchy. The irony is that Seth sees Basil as
a figure of culture, "a representative of Progress and the
New Age," "the personification of all that glittering,
intangible Western culture to which he aspired." The
novel creates, but never finally resolves, a condition of
equipoise between the progressive and modern and the

barbarian and primitive. Our sympathies never go out wholly either to Seal or to Seth. We admire Seal's resilience and power to survive in a recognisably barbarous world, and we see that Seth ignores something essential (Youkoumian says he needs a woman) and dies for this. But the deaths of Prudence and Seth turn us unexpectedly in favour of law and civilisation; the cannibal feast at which Basil inadvertently eats his fiancée ("I'd like to eat you," he has said to the misnamed Prudence) is an invention designed to outrage like nothing else in the earlier Waugh. It is the extreme of anarchy; the end of the novel recoils from it. Yet order is still untrue to experience, even when administered by the League of Nations mandate that governs Azania at the end, and worse it is dull, making the reader regret the loss of the exotic Azania of Seth's rule. So again the world of comic anarchy is made attractive by the comparison with formal order, yet again Waugh stops short of full commitment to it, offering with rather more than usual attentiveness the recommendations of the serious and the dull. This action in Azania is paralleled by the action in Mayfair, where the loss of the means and the will to be exotic and lively has produced a new seriousness. Only the amoral Youkoumian survives unscathed, another figure for the life-force which Waugh so intimately links with the comic spirit.

The plot of the novel is thus ostensibly a parable about the impossibility of imposing the order of progress upon the anarchy of life, but Waugh's tone is more than usually uncertain and this theme is not firmly sustained. Waugh has expressed his aims in a letter.

The story deals with the conflict of civilization, with all its attendant and deplorable ills, and barbarism. The plan of my book throughout was to keep the darker aspects of barbarism continually and unobtrusively present, a black and mischievous background against which the civilized and semi-civilized characters performed their parts; I wished it to be like the continuous, remote throbbing of hand drums, constantly audible, never visible. . . . I introduced the cannibal theme in the first chapter and repeated it in another key in the incident of the soldiers eating their boots, thus hoping to prepare the reader for the sudden tragedy when barbarism at last emerges from the shadows and usurps the stage.[27]

This hardly describes a comic plot, yet this is a comic novel, a novel of absurdities, conducted in a farcical world of double-cross and double-double-cross and depending for consistency on its dominant comic tone. Waugh's triumph is to handle very disparate materials, tones and events with such assurance as to draw them together in comedy, for his approach to this matter is tangential—so much so that it is difficult to find the centre of the action and be sure of the effect he is trying to produce. The novel begins with the revolution in Azania; only in Chapter III does Seal appear, so creating an ironic comment on the progress Seth is pursuing, and he is then treated with more detail than his role really warrants. Another such surprising device is the late introduction of Mildred Porch, the reformer, through whose eyes we see, very appropriately but still unexpectedly, the revolution deposing Seth. Similarly the scenes in the Embassies and the Birth Control Pageant are virtually episodes. Waugh's comic approach thus absolves him from conventional construction, enabling a wild fictional world and creating for those critics who seek to find a consistent vein of value or purpose in such books a difficult problem.

A Handful of Dust (1934) presents the problem in another form. The book, considered by many critics to be Waugh's best, is hardly open to direct moral interpretation, and shows his sympathies to be divided and capable of reconciliation only on the level of comedy, where everything takes on an essential absurdity. The hero, Tony Last, is something of a tragic figure—but he acts in a comic universe. Deceived by his wife, deprived of his son and heir in a hunting accident, he is compelled to leave Hetton, the Victorian Gothic mansion he loves, and ends up in the South American jungle reading Dickens to a mad settler ominously named Mr Todd. This is the first novel in which Waugh seems seriously engaged in the tragic situation of his hero; *Decline and Fall* and *Vile Bodies* are virtually novels without heroes, while in *Black Mischief* there are two heroes, both detached from the author, separation from his hero being an important aspect of Waugh's treatment of values and his means of access to comedy. But in *A Handful of Dust* Waugh appears to have invented a hero he can sympathise with, a country gentleman devoted to his squirarchical duties, suspicious of the Mayfair set, concerned only to establish his heir in his place; his tragedy, were he totally the tragic hero, would then be that he *is* the last, for his heir dies and his marriage is severed. However, this is not Waugh's treatment; Last's failure to be tragic in this way is at the heart of the book's interest. Farce is intermixed with seriousness in such a fashion as to turn the book in another direction, and there is a deep ambivalence in Waugh's approach which prevents us from accepting unreservedly the aristocratic myth with which he is associated. In this sense Last anticipates Guy Crouchback.

The action takes place in three social settings, two of them—that of Mayfair and the English countryside of Hetton—contrasted, the third that of the unsuccessful quest abroad by which Tony Last attempts to resolve these two. The urban detail is given rather differently from Waugh's other metropolitan settings; and it has a distinctly nineteen-thirtyish flavour. The sons and daughters of the aristocracy have only modest means, and the smart is also the slightly seedy; everyone is trying either to boost falling fortunes or win social esteem, and most of the Bright Young Things are now rather Middle-Aged Things who have to work for a living. They are a slightly lower set than that of the Lady Circumferences and Lady Metrolands, and they allow entrance to others rather more easily. They are modern and given to fads; osteopathy, fortune-telling (by reading feet), reducing diets and chromium plating in houses are in vogue; maisonette flats, the means by which Brenda facilitates her adultery, are fashionable; interior decoration is an important business. The young men go to Bratt's Club and stand for Parliament, while it is not odd for Brenda to pretend she is taking a course in economics. Restaurant lunches, open parties and night clubs, selling brandy in champagne bottles and employing amoral hostesses, are the entertainment. It is a world of broken marriages and affairs—"What fun everyone seems to be having," says Brenda when she hears the London gossip at Hetton, but it is made to seem far from being fun. And this whole world is administered by the busy Beavers—the novel opens with the picture of Mrs Beaver and her son John reflecting on the fortunate burning down of part of a great house which she will be commissioned to redecorate. Mrs Beaver, with a finger in every pie and a commission gained for everything, preys (like Polly Cockpurse) on the boredom and misfortunes of the aristocracy. Her son becomes Brenda's lover and the indirect agent of the destruction of Hetton. Like the beavers referred to in *Work Suspended* they "go through all the motions of damming an ancestral stream."[28]

The "ancestral stream" is associated with the house at Hetton, seat of the Lasts, but it is relatively modern, a Victorian Gothic pile rebuilt in 1864 from plans which, an aunt remarks, "must have been adapted by Mr. Pecksniff from one of his pupils' designs for an orphanage." Inconvenient, cold and strikingly uncomfortable, it

E

is difficult to keep up (the cost is an issue between Last
and Brenda). The London set find it horrible and dark
("I'd blow the whole thing sky-high," says Veronica)
but it is presented to us through Tony's feelings about it.
Tony, not an aristocrat (he has simply married one), has
espoused the aristocratic ideal as a part of a profound
Gothic dream, linked with childhood and adolescence—
"all these things with which he had grown up were a
source of constant delight and exultation to Tony; things
of tender memory and proud possession"—and with the
untouched night nursery in which all his dreams have
been bred. It is threatened by the fact that Brenda does
not share it, and finds the routine of opening fêtes and
playing *châtelaine* boring. She detests the house and is
supported in this by her London friends, who regard her
as "the imprisoned princess of fairy story." Waugh's own
sympathies do not, however, go entirely the way of Tony;
he is an urban novelist, attentive to the metropolitan part
of the action and fully engaged in the presentation of it.
He "places" Tony's agrarian and Utopian dream,
however much he values it; its childish quality makes it
pathetic as well as heroic, and it does destroy Tony "by
unfitting him to face up to a crisis in an adult way."[29]
Further, more of the action than is necessary simply for
conflict is devoted to winning sympathy for Brenda and
even her lover John Beaver; we see the indignations and
humiliations of Beaver's unemployed life, and the affair
itself is drawn with knowledge and some understanding.
Brenda says of Beaver:

> "He's second rate and a snob and, I should think, as
> cold as a fish, but I happen to have a fancy for him,
> that's all ... besides, I'm not sure he's *altogether*
> awful ... he's got that odious mother whom he
> adores ... and he's always been very poor. I don't
> think he's had a fair deal."[30]

The prevailing lax moral code and the general pleasure

felt in the affair by the London set ("Enjoy yourselves, bless you both," says Brenda's sister, and when she later disapproves for snobbish reasons plentiful encouragement comes from elsewhere) make Tony a ready victim. It is they who attempt to solve the problem by offering Tony an exotic mistress, Princess Abdul Akbar ("Anyway, this lets *you* out. You've done more than most wives would to cheer the old boy up," says Polly Cockpurse). Tony has less urbane standards ("He had got into the habit of loving and trusting Brenda"), but the *habit*, his extreme simplicity, and his failure to recognise Brenda's boredom contribute to the disaster, as does his Hetton cult, more admirable than any conviction among the London set, but still innocent, childish and a pretence:

> Brenda teased him whenever she caught him posing as an upright God-fearing gentleman of the old school and Tony saw the joke, but this did not at all diminish the pleasure he derived from his weekly routine, or his annoyance when the presence of guests suspended it.[31]

Thus Tony "insists on living in the Tennysonian world of *The Idylls of the King*. The standards of Victorian architecture and those of Victorian morality are, however, out of date. This Gothic world falls to pieces, and he comes to understand fear in his handful of dust."[32] Like many Waugh characters he lives in a fantasy, but his is exposed. The threat comes when the London set visit Hetton ("A thin mist lay breast high over the park; the turrets and battlements of the abbey stood grey and flat; the boiler man was hauling down the flag on the main tower") and the fantasy is destroyed by the death of his son and heir in a hunting accident, "nobody's fault."

This accident occurs during the visit of the mysterious Mrs Rattery, the Shameless Blonde, "totally denationalized, rich, without property or possessions," "very serene and distant," a *dea ex machina* who arrives by aeroplane and as suddenly disappears. By skilled management of all the threads of plot leading up to John Andrew's death, using great complication of point of view, Waugh establishes a pure, morally neutral accident, truly "nobody's fault." But the very pleasure Waugh has taken in the character of the boy, and the significance that he has for Tony's temporal hopes, his marriage and his dream means that we are conscious of a long chain of consequences. Here Mrs Rattery plays an important part for Waugh's intention, bringing a promise of order into a situation from which all order has, by authorial management, been abstracted. Like Mme Sosostris in *The Waste Land* (to which the title refers) she plays cards, this contrasting neatly with the fortune-telling that Brenda is attending at Lady Cockpurse's, where Mrs Northcote reads feet and Mrs Beaver takes, of course, a substantial commission. But Mrs Rattery's game is a search for order:

> (Mrs. Rattery sat intent over her game, moving little groups of cards adroitly backwards and forwards about the table like shuttles across a loom; under her fingers order grew out of chaos; she established sequence and precedence; the symbols before her became coherent, interrelated.)[33]

It is she who speaks to Tony of the consolations of religion which he has discarded. She administers over the end of one of his lives and the beginning of another, when heritage and marriage are taken from him (and for the first time in Waugh deprivation is a deeply painful occasion), by playing animal snap with him. Throughout this scene Waugh, maintaining his comic and exotic vein, walks a careful path between tenderness and outrage. The effect of the scene is to assert, from a standard higher than that represented by any of the characters, the emptiness of the whole world of the novel; another standard of judgment, only faintly and lightly referred to, is proposed, to act as a necessary guide through the work. In one way Waugh is less than authoritative, and relies rather on the reader's guesses, conveying a hint of some hidden order. The hint is contrived particularly by the use of Mrs Rattery, detached and mysterious, whose serenity indicates the extent of the chaos present and to come. But because the moral apparatus of the book is played down, to suggest the moral neutrality of its world, no more than a hint can be given. All the moral vocabulary of the novel is slangy and inadequate ("Hard cheese on Tony"); there is little ratiocination, for Waugh's method of rendering precludes it (he tends rather to use evocative symbolism or the pathetic fallacy); and the moral life of the characters is in any case judged totally from outside. Within the action moral justice is unlikely to be established. Those responses to the world of Hetton, Brenda and John Andrew which Tony feels so securely at the beginning of the novel are described in emotional terms; he feels "love," "trust," "tenderness," and "delight," emotions offered as in themselves matters for our sympathy. Later in the novel the words are repeated to ironic effect, their debasement being part of the chaos ("It's so like Brenda to trust everyone," "I don't think you have any right to take advantage of her generosity," and so on). The death of John Andrew has a similar moral bleakness ("Nobody's fault"). Yet its introduction into the novel is an effective and, indeed, really the only method of demonstrating the falsity of all the lives that are lead within it—including Last's own.

Thus, by satirical means and by the use of this central incident as a touchstone, a moral scale is introduced into the novel. It is, however, vague; the novel hardly shows decisively that affectionate marriage, the placing of the mother-son before the wife-lover relationship and an adequate recognition of the significance of death are the paramount values of the book. Waugh exerts as a comic writer a remarkable moral and emotional control over his readers, but we hardly emerge from his novels deeply engaged about the shocking conduct of his characters, or feeling that his satirical aim is reformatory. In the remarkable scene where Brenda, on discovering that the death being announced to her by Jock Grant-Menzies is not that of her lover but that of her son, says, "Oh, thank God," the effect is less outrageous than delicate, calling up other than moral responses; it appeals to truthfulness, to the tenderness between Beaver and Brenda that has genuinely been established, to the boredom that Brenda has felt at Hetton and the excitement of London which has made her happy again, and of course to the corruption that lies within her present situation. Of this last the news that Jock brings is an epiphany; Brenda herself has something of her situation revealed to her. And it is also, like Tony's response to the death, the revelation of a waste land, the justification of the title taken from T. S. Eliot, the indication that an event which is nobody's fault is indeed everybody's fault. The challenge to this world is a death which, for once, Waugh sees as a significant incident. This, indeed, is one of the differences between this novel and those which precede it—the death is *not* regarded as a comically arbitrary event in the stylised world of the comic novel (as, say, Messinger's is later on in the book).

Yet, though Waugh appeals outside the novel for a standard of value, he in no way takes less pleasure in his comic world. Indeed the development of the novel from this point is that the hero, Tony, moves into a realm of comedy, animality and chaos. Here all his expectations and values are steadily eroded, and he has finally to confront Mr Todd, the figure of death, himself. The second part of the action seems like a parody of the first, save that Tony now knows the kind of world he lives in:

for a month now he had lived in a world suddenly bereft of order; it was as though the whole reasonable and decent constitution of things, the sum of all he had

experienced or learned to expect, were an inconspicu-
ous, inconsiderable object mislaid somewhere on a
dressing table; no outrageous circumstance in which
he found himself, no new, mad thing brought to his
notice, could add a jot to the all encompassing chaos
that shrieked about his ears.[34]

The death of his son and the defection of his wife compel
him to give up his traditional idea of order; and he is
forced to enter (like Paul Pennyfeather) the realm of
chaos and irrationality. Like other Waugh heroes he is
deprived of all he possesses, but the dispossession comes
much later in the novel, is therefore much more painful
and much more significant, and is much more criticised
by the novelist. It is this that adds an odd dimension to
the book, and points to its ambiguity, for Waugh at once
seems to enjoy and to reject his comic world. The
comedy exposes delusions *as* delusions; Hetton turns into
Dr Messinger's city, not simply based on romantic folly
but, indeed, non-existent. Tony has to realise this:

His mind had suddenly become clearer on many points
that had puzzled him. A whole Gothic world had
come to grief . . . there was now no armour glittering
through the forest glades, no embroidered feet on the
green sward; the cream and dappled unicorns had
fled. . . .[35]

An intense romanticism tends to emerge when Waugh
grows more serious, but it does remain within the framework of the comedy, as we see in the fantastic mock-quest
with which the novel ends, a version of the traditional
journey of exploration taken by Englishmen when their
hearts are broken. In this journey Tony is at once the
scapegoat of the society, suffering for the sins of others,
and the scapegoat of the novelist, suffering because that
is habitual in his fictional world. Waugh has said that the
germ of the novel came out of the visit he paid to a lonely

settler in British Guinea, a religious maniac who could easily have kept him prisoner; and he describes in *Ninety-Two Days* his night's stay with this man, Mr Christie, who had been privileged to see the total assembly of the Elect in heaven and whose fantastic conversations "transformed that evening and raised it a finger's breadth above reality."[36] After using the idea of a man's being trapped by such a settler in the jungle for a short story, Waugh wanted to expand the incident.

> I wanted to discover how the prisoner got there, and eventually the thing grew into a study of other sorts of savages at home and the civilized man's helpless plight among them.[37]

Last's journey is thus from one jungle to another; and it largely repeats, in a different treatment, his experiences in the earlier part of the book. Hetton becomes Eldorado, or the Lost City in the jungle; London society becomes a savage tribal life; and Last himself becomes Candide, wretchedly innocent and yet seeing for the first time the truth. The cross-cutting from the jungle to London in the final pages not only enforces the similarity between these two worlds of savagery but shows that Last has understood and rejected the falsity of the London set. Yet his moment of knowledge about Brenda and Hetton ("His mind suddenly became clearer on many points that puzzled him") is not used by Last or the novelist in the conventional way, to help him take a better grip on actuality and so bring his fortunes to a happy outcome. It simply makes him aware that he has been living in a fantasy—and provokes a more intense dedication to fantasy as fantasy. The dream is taken up and used as a point or ideal by which the savagery of London can be indicted. Tony's quest is for a transfigured Hetton.

For some days now Tony had been thoughtless about

the events of the immediate past. His mind was occupied with the City, the Shining, the Many Watered, the Bright Feathered, the Aromatic Jam. He had a clear picture of it in his mind. It was Gothic in character, all vanes and pinnacles, gargoyles, battlements, groining and tracery, pavilions and terraces, a transfigured Hetton, pennons and banners floating on the sweet breeze, everything luminous and translucent; a coral citadel crowning a green hill top sown with daisies, among groves and streams; a tapestry landscape filled with heraldic and fabulous animals and symmetrical, disproportionate blossom.

The ship tossed and tunnelled through the dark waters towards this radiant sanctuary.[38]

But the whining of the dogs that form part of the animal cargo of the ship mocks the dream; and when, in an hallucination, Tony looks up from a game of animal snap to see the City it is neatly turned into the "indigenous architecture" of Mr Todd's hut. The "city is served," but it is the city of a living death. Tony's dream is higher than anything that is offered by the London set, but this Gothic paradise is not to be won on earth; it *is* a fantasy; all that is gained in life is death. In his fever Tony sees the point: "There is no City. Mrs Beaver has covered it with chromium plating and converted it into flats."[39] For this dream he has sacrificed the possibility of a charming affair and perhaps marriage with a Creole girl, even as Brenda (with whom, even in these final pages, we are sympathetically engaged) has sacrificed Hetton to an affair with Beaver and has now ended up with nothing. In the context of the ending the quest once again has higher claims, even though once again it closes in a handful of dust. But, as in *Black Mischief*, the novel ends by asserting the triumph of pedestrian reality. Relatives, the "impoverished Lasts," reign in modest circumstances at Hetton, now a silver-fox farm. Brenda marries Jock

Grant-Menzies; Mrs Beaver advises on the memorial for Tony, and remains in contact with the Lasts, her amoral capacity for survival being like that of Grimes and Youkoumian. The animals, which have mocked Tony (animal snap, etc.) throughout the book and brought about the death of his son, those animals so curiously linked in Waugh with the world of comic anarchy, are now in cages, tended by Teddy, who has taken on John Andrew's role as heir:

> The silver-fox farm was behind the stables; a long double row of wire cages; they had wire floors covered with earth and cinders to prevent the animals digging their way out. They lived in pairs; some were moderately tame but it was unwise to rely on them. . . .
>
> They ran up to the doors when they saw Teddy come with the rabbits. The vixen who had lost her brush seemed little the worse for her accident.
>
> Teddy surveyed his charges with pride and affection. It was by means of them that he hoped one day to restore Hetton to the glory that it had enjoyed in the days of his cousin Tony.[40]

The novel is far from being the reactionary tract that some critics have found it to be. Waugh has said of it that it "dealt entirely with behaviour. It was humanist and contained all that I had to say about humanism"[41]: but it is only humanist in the sense that none of the characters believes in God and all act for their own ends. What has Waugh to say about humanism? It is hard to know. For the novel is written in several different conventions, ranging from social satire and moral criticism to the grotesque fantasy of Last's quest, with its symbolic reference and its flavour of nightmare. Further, Waugh is engaged with all his characters, good as well as bad, so that their moral faults do not enduringly survive their comic existence and their comic role. The animal world of comedy again comes out as the energising principle of the action; and it is at this level rather than that of moral observation that the book is consistent. It is a novel beautifully organised and managed, all the threads of the action being drawn so carefully, all the preparation for coming events being given with such finesse, all the symbolic overtones being offered with such apparent consistency, that it is surprising to discover how little devoted Waugh is to his plot when, in an alternative ending, written for an American magazine, he allows Tony to return to Hetton with Brenda, who has lost her Beaver (now gone off in pursuit of Mrs Rattery), and shows him taking over Brenda's London flat in preparation for what are obviously to be *his* infidelities. Waugh's real concern is at the level of comic tone. This is an immensely funny book; the sermons of the Hetton vicar still believing himself a garrison chaplain, the magnificent farce of Tony's horribly respectable illicit weekend in Brighton with Winnie and her daughter, for the purposes of divorce, the grotesque comedy of Mr Todd and his Dickens-reading slaves, all assert the primacy of the comic invention and the place of the tragic events within their framework. Animality and amorality triumph not simply because the world works against the Tony Lasts, but because Waugh's vision of the world is for his early fiction enlisted on the side of comic anarchy. The remarkable thing about the book is how much we are engaged with Tony, care about his dream, take him seriously, within this mode. Suffering is now implicated in absurdity; the novel is, like *Tristram Shandy*, a tragi-comedy, and the shape of its plot points not toward the restoration of order but toward the penance paid by the hero in, and for, such a world. By a presentation alternately amusing and tender he creates an amiable bond with the reader in which Last is involved. Because of the special sanctity given to Tony's myth of Hetton—the innocent aristocratic paradise, the prelapsarian estate so linked with childhood and so patently doomed in the lapsed world of comedy—his role as victim is intensified. Thus Waugh embodies in him an attitude and a pattern of values that he shows to be at once desirable and insufficient to face the world about us and the death it contains, an ironic device of presentation much used in modern novels to limit the assertiveness of any offered values. These in turn challenge the values of the London set, not totally but comparatively, and establish for almost the first time a centre of incorruptibility in one of his novels.

In 1936 Waugh collected a number of short stories (and the alternative ending to *A Handful of Dust*, here titled "By Special Request") into a volume called *Mr. Loveday's Little Outing and Other Sad Stories*. Set either among the rural aristocracy or in the London of Mayfair or of journalism and fiction-writing, these stories, written over a number of years and fairly modest in intention, are most interesting for the way they fill out Waugh's fictional world, showing his obsession with madness, his interest in the exploitation of one person by another, and his fondness for re-using characters from his earlier fiction. His next novel, published in 1938, is *Scoop: A Novel About Journalists*, in which he turns from the complex handling of *A Handful of Dust* to a simpler style of presentation. *Scoop* is high farce, and abounds in burlesque passages, mistaken identities, stylised misunderstandings, characters simplified and heightened to comic proportions. It in no way engages the reader in such sympathies as *A Handful of Dust* has required, and though there is some similarity of material—once again there are two worlds, one agrarian and associated with a country house, the other metropolitan and international and associated with a London changing yet further into a city of demolition and traffic jams—the treatment is lighter, more detached. The action, episodic even for Waugh, develops largely in the world of international politics, international journalism, international finance and international intrigue (and against these things

Waugh's satirical intentions are directed), as it is encountered by one of his most innocent heroes. William Boot, like Paul Pennyfeather, is a simple figure, and like Paul he is removed from his natural setting, undergoes a series of fantastic adventures, a ritual of involvement, and then returns to that setting virtually unchanged. He has handled large sums of money, been in the seats of power, had great knowledge and influence, fallen in love, but none of these things have lasted and, more important, he has never really understood them, so that his return to his retreat is an indication of his inadequacy as well as of his worth. Instead of the careful interpenetration of London and Hetton we get in this novel two distinct and opposed worlds, but drawn largely for their burlesque effects. One is the world of Lord Copper, Mr Baldwin, Fascism, Communism and war, a world of power and influence peopled by comic figures like Mrs Stitch, driving her small car over pavements, through parks and into gentlemen's lavatories, John Courteney Boot, the urban novelist who should have gone to Ishmaelia, and the inhabitants (Mr Salter and so on) of the London office of *The Daily Beast*. But if this world is full of follies, so is the second world, that of Boot Magna Hall, that depressed rural retreat where William lives amid eccentric relatives and equally eccentric servants, writing a bi-weekly half-column on Nature ("LUSH PLACES, edited by William Boot, Countryman") for *The Daily Beast*. The two worlds are brought into full contact when, by a comic sequence of mistaken identities, William is asked to cover a crisis in the East African country of Ishmaelia. An innocent abroad ("the moment he left the confines of Boot Magna he found himself in a hostile and foreign world"), he wants nothing save to keep his *Lush Places* column ("Feather-footed through the splashy fen passes the questing vole . . .") and go on living at home. There is one point of detachment from it, a secret ambition that has niggled him for fifteen years:

He did, very deeply, long to go up in an aeroplane. It was a wish so far from the probabilities of life at Boot Magna that William never spoke of it . . . away from people and cities to a region of light and void and silence. . . .

Another lush place, in fact. But he is forcibly detached, through a symbolic sequence of events which deprive him of his clothes and involve him in an encounter with a pageboy whose face is "of ageless evil." He is equipped with a meaningless jumble of explorer's luggage, meets uncomprehendingly the emissaries of the two warring sides (a Fascist Negro and a Communist Negro, neither actually citizens of Ishmaelia but part of the world alignments which are the real cause of the trouble there), and finally makes his way, in a series of farcical episodes, to Ishmaelia, a hitherto happy commonwealth:

Desert, forest and swamp, frequented by furious nomads, protect its approaches from those more favoured regions which the statesmen of Berlin and Geneva have put to school under European masters. An inhospitable race of squireens cultivate the highlands and pass their days in the perfect leisure which those peoples alone enjoy who are untroubled by the speculative or artistic itch.[42]

However, modern passions have been aroused, political sympathies have grown up in the world outside, and above all the press has been alerted and sent its emissaries to Ishmaelia, so creating a crisis which is bound to turn into a war. Among this press colony, riven by jealousies and professional pride, and with a well-developed efficiency at inventing news should none happen to be in the offing, Boot settles. He discovers, through an old school friend at the British Legation, the presence of a Russian emissary, but this is not news; another correspondent has sent out a similar but wholly invented story

which has "scooped" him. Then, by a series of accidents
and by unprofessional inefficiency, he moves from the hotel
where the pressmen are staying, fails to go on a press
expedition to a non-existent town, begins an affectionate
relationship with a girl from whom, out of kindness, he
buys a bag of stones for £20—and so discovers the truth
of the whole situation. Ishmaelia is in crisis because
Russia and Germany are competitively in pursuit of gold
which has been found there.

Boot has also fallen in love with Kätchen, the "wife"
of the German speculator whose stones reveal the
situation:

> He was in love. It was the first time in twenty-three
> years; he was suffused and inflated and tipsy with love.
> It was believed at Boot Magna, and jocularly com-
> mented on from time to time, that an attachment
> existed between him and a neighbouring Miss
> Caldicote; it was not so. He was a stranger alike to the
> bucolic jaunts of the hay field and the dark and costly
> expeditions of his Uncle Theodore. For twenty-three
> years he had remained celibate and heart-whole;
> land-bound. Now for the first time he was far from
> shore, submerged among deep waters, below wind and
> tide, where huge trees raised their spongy flowers and
> monstrous things without fur or feather, wing or foot,
> passed silently, in submarine twilight. A lush place.[43]

While Boot is immersed in this new submarine world, all
the main events of the action happen in rapid succession
and on a single day. He cables—it is "a moment of
history"—the news that a Russian *coup* is taking place,
once again without realising its significance ("NOTHING
MUCH HAS HAPPENED EXCEPT TO THE PRESIDENT WHO HAS
BEEN IMPRISONED IN HIS OWN PALACE BY REVOLUTIONARY
JUNTA . . ."); then, when the complications of the plot
have been explained to him, he resolves to "do down" the
plotters:

Dimly at first, then in vivid detail, he foresaw a
spectacular, cinematographic consummation, when
his country should rise chivalrously to arms; Bengal
Lancers and kilted highlanders invested the heights of
Jacksonburg; he at their head burst open the prison
doors. . . . Kätchen fluttered towards him like a
wounded bird and he bore her in triumph to Boot
Magna. . . . Love, patriotism, zeal for justice and
personal spite flamed within him as he sat at his type-
writer and began his message.[44]

Kätchen's "husband" returns, and he contrives both
their escapes, so ending his incipient love-affair. The
lush place is lost. Then the Soviet State of Ishmaelia is
declared, provoking him to pray to the great-crested
grebe (whose name, substituted by his sister in an article
originally about badgers, has caused his journey):

He bowed his head.
"Oh, great crested grebe," he prayed, "maligned
fowl, have I not expiated the wrong my sister did you;
am I still to be an exile from the green places of my
heart? Was there not even in the remorseless dooms of
antiquity a god from the machine?"
He prayed without hope.[45]

Immediately an aeroplane appears and drops a para-
chutist; the *deus ex machina* appears once more. This time
he is the mysterious adventurer Mr Baldwin who neatly
resolves the action in the best possible way. This arrogant
conceit is typical of the way Waugh belittles his plot and
reassures the reader that this is an invented world, as he
does when Paul Pennyfeather mysteriously disappears:
might and right triumph, Boot gets his story, and returns
to England a popular hero. All that remains is for the
world of Boot Magna to triumph finally over the world
of politics, Lord Copper and London ("that atrocious
city"). Lord Copper requires William at a banquet and

sends Mr Salter, the provincial Londoner who has throughout been set against William the provincial countryman, in pursuit; he undergoes a series of rural misfortunes and ends up at a ghastly feast at Boot Magna. Uncle Theodore goes to Lord Copper's banquet and joins his staff, so fulfilling his more urbane ambitions, and William ends the novel happily writing another *Lush Places* ("maternal rodents pilot their furry brood through the stubble"). But has he been successful? His lush place is after all too innocent, and not inviolable, as the last line underscores: "Outside the owls hunted maternal rodents and their furry brood." And desirable as Boot Magna is, it is in the last stages of change and decay, particularly decay:

The immense trees which encircled Boot Magna Hall, shaded its drives and rides, and stood . . . singly and in groups about the park, had suffered, some from ivy, some from lightning, some from the various malignant disorders that vegetation is heir to, but all principally from old age. . . . Sap ran thin and slow; a gusty night always brought down a litter of dead timber.[46]

William is in a similar condition. To this he has sentimentally returned, and he has preserved his standard of judgment, the standard of Nannie Bloggs. He is the most successful, least suffering of all Waugh's heroes: but he has lost his love and the "new world" that went with it, and his victory is a small one. His innocence is that of the simpleton hero who triumphs over the strange, unattractive world of power politics through his ignorance, his kindliness and his dream of inviolable lush places. But these are also the realm of true affection and love as well as detachment, and are not without their cruelties. Boot Magna may be a sufficient retreat for the heroic innocent, but it does not solve the problem of the animal cruelties of the world, being simply a retirement from it.

The innocent heroes of Waugh's early novels are used

F

(as are his recurrent *milieux* and his favourite contrasts, particularly of city and country) in many different ways. None of them, however, are used (as Salinger uses Holden Caulfield) to convey an ideal of innocence, simplicity and childlike questioning which challenges the world about; they are too innocent, romantic and self-engaged for that, and Waugh is more urbane. The innocence of Last and Boot is rebellious, but we are never sufficiently engaged with them as culture-heroes, never sufficiently free from enjoyment of the world they rebel against, to find this the point of the novel. Usually they do penance for the comic world they enter, an urbane, anarchic world in which innocence cannot be expected to survive. But Waugh's treatment of Boot is very different from that of Paul Pennyfeather. The innocence which was to some extent Paul's weakness is largely William's strength. Paul rejects a world that Waugh understands and delights in; William rejects a world that Waugh, over four novels, has learned to be suspicious of, and so emerges relatively intact and with much of the reader's sympathy. Waugh's use of London, a steadily changing city with its vile bodies increasingly engaged in business and politics, has slowly altered (it has a fascinating thirty-year history in his novels). It is perhaps for this reason that, with *Work Suspended*, he begins to develop a new tone and a new realism, in which the world of comic absurdity and anarchy, in all its animalism and madness, is brought much closer to everyday experience, is tamed and loses much of its early joy.

REFERENCES

1. *D.F.*, p. 52.
2. *D.F.*, p. 53.
3. *D.F.*, p. 84.
4. *D.F.*, p. 114.
5. *D.F.*, pp. 136–7.

6. *D.F.*, p. 140.
7. *D.F.*, p. 190.
8. *D.F.*, p. 208.
9. *D.F.*, p. 231.
10. *D.F.*, p. 232.

11. Eric Linklater, *The Art of Adventure*, 1947, pp. 44–58.

12. *D.F.*, p. 227.

13. A. E. Dyson, "Evelyn Waugh and the Misteriously Disappearing Hero," 1960, p. 74.

14. *D.F.*, p. 138.

15. *D.F.*, p. 139.

16. D. S. Savage, "The Innocence of Evelyn Waugh," 1947, pp. 34–46.

17. James Hall, "The Other Post-War Rebellion: Evelyn Waugh Twenty-Five Years After," 1961, pp. 187 ff.

18. Patrick Balfour, *Society Racket*, p. 70.

19. *V.B.*, p. 127.

20. *V.B.*, p. 185.

21. *V.B.*, p. 118.

22. Martin Green, "Meaning and Delight in Evelyn Waugh."

23. *B.M.*, p. 225.

24. *B.M.*, p. 70.

25. *B.M.*, p. 18.

26. *B.M.*, p. 29.

27. Stopp, p. 32.

28. *W.S.*, p. 238.

29. Peter Green, "Du Côté de Chez Waugh," 1961, p. 95.

30. *H.D.*, p. 51.

31. *H.D.*, pp. 26–7.

32. DeVitis, p. 31.

33. *H.D.*, p. 117.

34. *H.D.*, p. 147.

35. *H.D.*, p. 163.

36. *N—T.D.*, p. 88.

37. "Fan-Fare," 1946, p. 58.

38. *H.D.*, p. 173.

39. *H.D.*, p. 225.

40. *H.D.*, p. 240.

41. "Fan-Fare," 1946, p. 60.

42. *S.*, p. 79.

43. *S.*, pp. 135–6.

44. *S.*, p. 167.

45. *S.*, p. 178.

46. *S.*, pp. 15–16.

CHAPTER IV

THE LATER NOVELS

In an article in *Life* in 1946, Waugh drew attention to the fact that his work was about to change in order to represent a new interest in stylistic and religious matters.[1] Readers of Waugh were, however, conscious of technical development rather earlier, with the publication of his novel-fragment *Work Suspended* in 1941. Change is indeed the theme of this novel, a book about altering social and artistic conditions, about a man who has to revise a settled and ordered life because he is deprived of the things that make it possible, and about the acceleration of political events which finally, in fact, prevent Waugh's completing the work. In a postscript describing the effect of the outbreak of war on his life and fiction, the first-person narrator, John Plant, a writer of detective stories, writes:

> My father's death, the abandonment of my home, my quickening love of Lucy, my literary innovations, my house in the country—all these had seemed to presage a new life. The new life came, not by my contrivance ... all our lives, as we had constructed them, quietly came to an end. Our story, like my novel, remained unfinished—a heap of neglected foolscap at the back of a drawer.[2]

The action of the book, in its two completed sections (entitled "A Death" and "A Birth"), takes place in the final months of peace, mainly in London, a serious London of vanishing houses and rising flats, of commercial travellers and Communist sympathisers. The members of the Waugh "set" are marrying, buying houses, growing older. Basil Seal, one of the most rounded and least farcical of Waugh's characters, plays a minor part, but the old creatures of burlesque have disappeared, their role being carried by the excellent comic invention of Atwater, the self-dramatising commercial traveller who has run down Plant's father in his car, and so feels that he can claim relationship with Plant. His shabby-genteel manners and fantasies are drawn from life with little exaggeration; his place in the novel stems from his oddity and his role as Plant's *alter ego*. While Waugh's earlier novels are self-contained comic inventions, adapting the convention of the innocent *picaro* with illusory expectations in an illusory world, in this book Plant— significantly Waugh's first first-person narrator—is offered with new seriousness and a new range of feeling. Obligations and affections are represented as serious matters. Plant is concerned with accurate delineation in a book in which death, birth, love and duty involve genuine suffering. The contingent world of farcical cruelty is transformed into the necessary world of feeling, with all its deeply felt demands:

To write of someone loved, of oneself loving, above all of oneself being loved—how can these things be done with propriety? How can they be done at all?[3]

Plant's life is in fact affected by the impact of two powerfully represented emotional events. His father dies, and he has to come to terms with the man who slays him, the slayer representing the triumph of a new kind of life over the old. He also falls in love with a married woman, and has to answer to a feeling that violates an essential modesty and solitude. When the novel opens Plant is a comfortable solitary living in Fez, writing successfully and engaging in only two social activities—occasional dinner with the Consul and regular arranged visits to a girl named Fatima in the *quartier toléré*. This life is interrupted by a police raid on the *quartier* which violates the privacy of Fez on which he depends—"I set a price on Modesty which those of ampler virtues might justly regard as fanciful"—and by the street accident which kills his father and so violates his security in a deeper way. Returning home to supervise the destruction of his father's house, much reduced in value by the development in its area of unsaleable flats, he finds a new world and is forced to recall the old. Plant has disliked possessions but now, deprived of a place "to hang my hat," he is conscious that they shape a way of life. He recollects with no more than a distant affection or mild nostalgia his father's values—those of "a dogmatic atheist of the old-fashioned cast," rejecting all popular opinions and regarding all public life as a conspiracy for the destruction of his class. His father's views, views that have been too easily associated with Waugh, are not Plant's:

"There are only three classes in England now— politicians, tradesmen and slaves. . . . Seventy years ago the politicians and the tradesmen were in alliance; they destroyed the gentry by destroying the value of land; some of the gentry became politicians themselves, others tradesmen; out of what was left they created a new class into which I was born, the moneyless, land-less, educated gentry who managed the country for them. My grandfather was a Canon of Christ Church, my father was in the Bengal Civil Service. All the capital they left their sons was education and moral principle. Now the politicians are in alliance with the slaves to destroy the tradesmen. They don't need to bother about us. We are extinct already. I am a Dodo," he used to say, defiantly staring at his audience. "You, my poor son, are a petrified egg."[4]

Symbolically, he is run over by a commercial traveller, his house is replaced by a bad block of flats; and Plant's problem is to come to terms with the modern world. His friends have married; some profess left-wing opinions, but manifest a kind of nostalgia for the style of living they, and Plant, emphatically reject in practical affairs. They have an appearance, as a set, of cynicism and unseriousness, and in this they are challenged by Lucy, the wife of one of Plant's friends, with whom he falls in love. Lucy belongs to a slightly younger generation and her ideal is not modesty—"in friendship [she] had all the modesty of the naked savage":

> There was little love and no trust at all between any of my friends. Moreover, we were bored; each knew the other so well that it was only by making our relationship into a kind of competitive parlour game that we kept it alive at all. . . . That was what I meant by friendship at the age of thirty-four, and Lucy, finding herself without preparation among people like myself, had been disconcerted. . . . She could not cope with the attack and defence, deception and exposure, which was our habitual intercourse. Anything less than absolute intimacy embarrassed her.[5]

Plant, the traditionalist retiring to the country, and Roger, the parlour Communist who is Lucy's husband, are alike challenged by her, for she is capable of confronting the ugly world, while the "set" are not. Attached to a decaying ideal of *bourgeois* art, they have still left unsatisfied "those wistful, half-romantic, half-aesthetic, peculiarly British longings" once expressed in poetry and turn not to Nature but to buildings—"almost any buildings, but particularly those in the classical tradition, and, more particularly, in its decay." But Lucy, with her challenging pregnancy, has a natural animalism characterised by Humboldt's Gibbon, a creature that she and Plant visit together at the London zoo:

> "If I have a boy I'll call him Humboldt," she said. "Do you know that before I was born, so Aunt

Maureen says, my mother used to sit in front of a
Flaxman bas-relief to give me ideal beauty. . . ."[6]

The gibbon suggests all the anarchy and barbarism
Plant is trying to exclude. But his attempt to take up with
the Lucys and the Atwaters is important, for here we
have a theme Waugh is to develop, that of a man of
Waugh's own situation, closely and sympathetically
observed, who knows himself to be a product of a simpler
time, yet strives to reconcile himself with the disorderly
and unattractive modern world, a world political,
destructive of traditional values, and genuinely challenging. Plant is not trying to cut himself off, but to meet it;
like Waugh himself, he has a sense of period and of
obligation to the new generation which itself tends to
exclude him. This requires a new presentation. In the
earlier novels social delineation, though accurately and
sharply given, is subordinate to fantasy; here and in later
novels this is reversed. Thus while the earlier novels tend,
so to speak, to start from the world of anarchy and put to
the test the world of order, the later ones tend rather to
start from order and judge anarchy in terms of it. The
myth of the past begins to grow, to appear in the novels
as an ideal prelapsarian world, but it would be wrong to
suggest that Waugh is fictionally entirely committed to it.

Put Out More Flags, published in 1942, is set in the
period of the Phoney War, "in that odd, dead period
before the Churchillian renaissance, which people called
at the time the Great Bore War." It deals, as Waugh's
dedicatory letter to Randolph Churchill goes on to
say:

with a race of ghosts, the survivors of the world we both
knew ten years ago . . . where my imagination still
fondly lingers. . . . These characters are no longer
contemporary in sympathy; they were forgotten even
before the war; but they lived on delightfully in holes
and corners and, like everyone else, they have been

disturbed in their habits by the rough intrusion of current history.[7]

Like any writer particularly committed to a generation, Waugh has to encounter the problem of superannuation, and the "ghosts"—survivors from the earlier novels, Basil Seal, Alistair Trumpington, Peter Pastmaster and others—are brought up to date by confrontation with new circumstances and a new literary style, one in which the fond, lingering imagination plays a greater part. Waugh has much the same problem as Seal, who reappears as anti-hero:

> Like Nazi diplomacy Basil's use of appeasement, agitation and blackmail postulated for success a peace-loving, orderly and honourable world in which to operate. In the new, busy, secretive, chaotic world which developed during the first days of the war, Basil for the first time in his life felt himself at a disadvantage. It was like being in Latin America at a time of upheaval, and, instead of being an Englishman, being oneself a Latin American.[8]

Similarly the novelist himself has always assumed an orderly and controllable universe beyond the fiction, and when the real world becomes as anarchistic as the fictional, he is forced to represent an order against which anarchy can be measured. Thus we are made to understand that there is a civilisation to be defended against the "small and envious mind, a meanly ascetic mind, a creature of the conifers [which] was plotting the destruction of [Barbara Sothill's] home," and by the end of the novel even the delinquent Basil has had, in a mood of responsible irresponsibility, to accept this—"There's only one serious occupation for a chap now, and that's killing Germans. I have an idea I shall rather enjoy it." In war the pirate becomes respectable; anarchy becomes crudely linked with the good cause; the claims of order intensify.

But this nod toward respectability in the final pages permits the romp before it; the Phoney War setting allows the Feast of Misrule of the main action, which is, like Bratt's week when Alistair Trumpington commits adultery, "a Saturnalia when the laws did not run," and in which Basil plays the part of the affable rogue creating flux and injustice in a still too orderly universe. Barbara Sothill, his sister, thinks he has needed a war—"I believe it's what he's been waiting for all these years." Her view is, however, as illusory as those of Lady Seal and Angela Lyne. Lady Seal sees him as the son she can offer her country; Angela sees him as, quite simply, dead ("Best thing really for all concerned"). Basil really fits none of these cases: "Rupert Brooke, Old Bill, the Unknown Soldier—thus three fond women saw him, but Basil . . . fell short and wide of all these ideals." He is for most of the novel the cynical opposite of all such standards; he has a vague idea of doing special service, which seems an appropriate pursuit for rascals, but he really wants to be one of the hard-faced men who did well out of the War. Though when Alistair Trumpington joins the army and refuses to become an officer his wife Sonia explains that he feels that war might have been avoided had he had less fun in earlier years—"He went into the ranks as a kind of penance or whatever it's called that religious people are always supposed to do"—this is not the main moral point of the novel, but part of one of the two contrasting plots. One, a plot about anarchy, with Basil using three hideous evacuees for blackmailing purposes in a private version of the billeting scheme, sits side by side with a plot about the penitential warriors, each giving occasion for different kinds of burlesque and farce. The book is a very various one, with a wide range of characters and locales, ranging from Barbara Sothill's country house at Malfrey, which sees one war, to the bohemian world around Poppet Green and Ambrose Silk, which sees another, dominated by the question whether Parsnip and Pimpernel, two left-wing writers who have gone to America, have done the right thing. The book contains as much excellent comedy as the earlier novels, but since the anarchistic world is that of the War, rather than of Waugh's own making, certain gestures to duty are imposed upon the work and shape the action.

The nature of the pressure of war is implied by one of the epigraphs to the book: "A little injustice in the heart can be drowned by wine; but a great injustice in the world can be drowned only by the sword (Chang Ch'ao)." A considerable part of the action is concerned with the movement from living individually for the single injustice in the heart, to living corporately for the great injustice in the world. Ambrose Silk, the Jewish homosexual aesthete and writer finally betrayed by Seal, believes in the ideal of the Chinese kingdom in which the warrior is inferior to the scholar. His ideal is "cenobitic" (he appears to misuse this word, which refers to a dweller in a convent or community, to characterise the life of lonely dedication); the world is becoming "conventual." Silk, tricked by Seal into writing a story of Fascist sympathies and so compelled to escape, dressed as a priest, to Ireland, discovers that he does in fact yearn for the world of effort and action "the dark, nomadic strain in his blood, the long heritage of wandering and speculation, allowed him no rest"[9]—but he remains outside the new community of war. The cruelty of his betrayal by his old friend Seal is that, though he represents what war must put aside, the event is to Seal's personal advantage, is a ritual of supersession—Basil makes a new mistress replace the monogram on the *crêpe de chine* underclothes Silk has left in his haste with his own. The husband of Basil's permanent mistress Angela Lyne is similarly a scapegoat; Cedric too is an aesthete ("he only cared about Russian ballet and baroque architecture") suspicious of the army. He however joins the action, to become victim of the military theme as Ambrose is of the civilian one. He enters battle believing in the individual:

> The great weapons of modern war did not count in single lives. . . . No one had anything against the individual; as long as he was alone he was safe and free; there's danger in numbers; divided we stand, united we fall, thought Cedric, striding happily towards the enemy, shaking from his boots all the frustration of corporate life. He did not know it, but he was thinking exactly what Ambrose had thought when he announced that culture must cease to be conventual and become cenobitic.[10]

But the individualists must be sacrificed and he dies unnecessarily in battle. There is another ritual of super-session; Basil and Angela plan marriage ("I knew we needed a death," says Angela and Basil comments "The dog it was that died . . ."). Thus Barbara Sothill is right— Basil needs a war, in order for him to supersede the old individualists. Aesthetes give way to cads, men of taste to men of action. A cruel philosophy, but the aesthetes are treated sympathetically, like Plant; Ambrose's anti-political stand, Cedric's Gothic taste, are part of Waugh himself. However, as the booby Sir Joseph Mainwaring says in the last lines, "There's a new spirit abroad." It is the spirit of simple, schoolboyish militarism (Peter Pastmaster and Alistair Trumpington, "adorable small boys") and Seal's new willingness to kill Germans. But it is also the spirit of the cad and the racketeer, of Seal and his two *alter egos*, Mr Todhunter and Colonel Plum. The ending has a note of irony, and Waugh's sympathies are again not easily fixed. War, demanding recognition as a reality, reinforces the schoolboys and the cads, demotes the aesthetes and the outsiders, and suggests a new and uncomfortable principle of order in a breaking world. Though both Silk and Seal are born out of their time, both are moral freebooters, and both are, in a sense, part of the same Waugh scene, figures of life's comic anarchy; Seal's superior power is that he can adapt to a world "absolutely uninhabitable for anyone of civilized taste" and he is played off against Silk, who is drawn to some degree tragically. Seal is also "no good." The ending is thus an ironic restatement of normality after the comic world has been dissolved by a death that, like those of Prudence and Seth, brings home the harshness of that world. As Angela says to Seal, "One can't expect anything to be perfect now."

Brideshead Revisited: The Sacred and Profane Memories of Captain Charles Ryder (1945) is probably Waugh's best known novel. It is, in many quarters, his least liked; according to Waugh's Preface to the revised edition (1960), it "lost me such esteem as I once enjoyed among my contemporaries and led me into an unfamiliar world of fan-mail and press photographers." It was written in the period of soya beans and Basic English and so has

a kind of gluttony, for food and wine, for the splendours of the recent past, and for rhetorical and ornamental language, which now with a full stomach I find distasteful. . . . It seemed then that the ancestral seats which were our chief national artistic achievement were doomed to decay and spoliation like the monasteries in the sixteenth century. So I piled it on rather.[11]

Most critics seem to agree that he piled it on rather. Rose Macaulay has complained that the novel contains an "adolescent surrender to glamour, whether to the glamour of beauty, food, rank, love, church, society or fine writing," and that, though there is much wit and subtly precise writing, it develops a disconcerting "luxury of bloom"— "Love, the English aristocracy, and the Roman Catholic Church, combine to liquefy a style that should be dry."[12] Donat O'Donnell, a more tendentious critic, complains that the author's purpose, which is "an attempt to trace the divine purpose in a pagan world," is obscured by a deep English romanticism and by a heresy—"In Mr. Waugh's theology, the love of money is not only not the root of all evil, it is a preliminary form of the love of God"—in which Catholicism has been superimposed upon "a fixed intolerant mythology" about the embattled English upper classes.[13] Professor Kermode finds that the book equates historically the English aristocratic and the Catholic traditions, that it contains Waugh's fullest treatment of the idea of the Catholic City, which must be defended from within, and that in consequence

> the operation of divine grace seems to be confined to those who say "chimney-piece" and to the enviable poor. Hooper and his brothers may be hard to bear, they may be ignorant of the City, but it seems outrageous to damn them for their manners.[14]

Brideshead Revisited is certainly at once a romance about the decline of a country house, involving the family who live in it and the tradition of conduct and living with which they are associated, and an explicitly Catholic novel with a religious theme—"the operation of divine grace on a group of diverse but closely connected characters."[15] It represents Waugh's first serious attempt to express his Catholicism fictionally, and contains his most frankly romantic picture of the Catholic history of England, a history in which generations of the faithful have had upon them a special mark of destruction:

> These men must die to make a world for Hooper; they were the aborigines, vermin by right of law, to be shot off at leisure so that things might be safe for the travelling salesman, with his polygonal pince-nez, his fat wet hand-shake, his grinning dentures.

Waugh's main subject is however the instability of the world, the failure of human aspiration, the impermanence of any human edifice, the omnipresence of suffering. The Flytes, like their ancestors the Catholic recusants, are

agents of a remotely working providence, and manifest
the unfashionable virtue of self-abnegation, so exposing
Ryder's own inadequacies. The main image in the book
is that of the avalanche which by destroying also purifies.
It is an image at once of anarchy and the Grace that so
often, for Catholic writers, has an aspect of destruction
and catastrophe[16] because it destroys the secure personality. The avalanche, linked with the social catastrophe that breaks up the joined worlds of youth, idyllic
Brideshead and the places of escape, is associated with
other images of disaster (some echoed from earlier books)
—the closing in of the jungle, the permanent threat of
war, the destruction and dereliction of great buildings,
the entry of politics into all walks of life, the fragmenta-
tion of the social order and the rise of a brash new class.
Waugh excels at images of this kind, isolating the
significant object or person—the Grimes-like figure who
appears at the Ryders' shipboard party and is arrested at
the end of the voyage; the slowly melting ice swan; the
tortoise with the jewel in its back—in a world rich in
objects, people and sensations. The contingent world of
earlier novels, because it is not susceptible to moral
ordering, finds a providential though not a total answer
in Catholicism, with what Lady Marchmain calls its
poetry, its Alice-in-Wonderland side. Here avalanche
and anarchy can create love, as Cordelia says: "I've seen
so much suffering in the last few years; there's so much
coming for everybody soon. It's the spring of love. . . ."
A purpose works itself out in the book, but independently
of the ambitions of any of the characters:

Something quite remote from anything the builders
[of Brideshead] had intended, had come out of their
work, and out of the fierce little human tragedy in
which I played; something none of us thought at the
time; a small red flame. . . .[17]

This is the flame in the chapel that symbolises the

continuance of faith, and it is lit out of tragedy and suffering. *Brideshead Revisited*, the most ambitious and extended of Waugh's novels to date, develops many of the powers Waugh has already established. An intensely social novel, it gives the detailed social history of the period from the end of the First World War to the middle of the Second, covering political and social changes, alterations in taste and manners, the decline of traditional moral values, the rise of the *bourgeoisie* in society and of the proletariat in social influence, and also such specific historical events as the General Strike, the Spanish Civil War and Hitler's rise to power. The action is geographically broad, covering much of Western Europe and touching North and South America. Further, despite the disturbing "liquidity" of the narrative prose on occasion, and the substitution of sentimental softness for comic hardness, Waugh makes use of a remarkable variety of tones (as when the delightful comedy of Bridey's announcement of his engagement suddenly shifts into his decisive criticism of Julia's moral conduct). And the action, widely extended in time, geography, character and tone, is also extended in another way—it is presented with a remarkable absence of moral comment and of *leads*. It is thus a fable about providence and also a novel of sentiments—that is, we are less interested in the moral conduct of the characters than in the emotions (love, nostalgia, affection, prejudice, faith) that explain it. The psychological development of the individual characters is handled with care and perception—Sebastian's escapism and alcoholism, Blanche's homosexuality, Lord Marchmain's Byronic self-indulgence—and this should remind us that the book should be seen within the romance *genre*, a *genre* characteristically tending toward melodrama, idyll, poetic presentation, symbolism or allegory and psychological analysis.

These qualities are facilitated by Waugh's complex use of a first-person narrator and an indirect chronology.

Presented as a first-person retrospect or memoir by a figure who is other than the novelist ("I am not I"), and for whom the whole inner action has personal significance, the book opens with a prologue in which the narrator reveals his current wartime situation and his disaffection with the world and the army; then recounts retrospectively his relations with the house at Brideshead; and ends with an epilogue showing the effect of the recollection on his spirits and understanding. This chronology enables Waugh to invest the central passages of recollection with an intensity of feeling they could not otherwise have, and make them relevant to later days when narrator and society have radically changed. The scenes set in the present not only frame the book but clarify its meaning, serving to introduce (as do, for instance, the scenes with Lockwood in *Wuthering Heights*) the romantic agents initially from the point of view of drab normality, and set off their behaviour as a ritual of a Giant Race before the Flood. The drab "normality" of the present is at once the *real* truth, criticising the richness of the inner tale, and the *empty* truth, criticised by it. The "present" Charles Ryder is an alien, disillusioned, suffering, separated from "Arcadia." Yet he has been an alien in Arcadia too, the ritual act of marriage to Julia, which would have allowed him entry, being interrupted in the final pages. His relationship to the Flytes is the main theme of the novel and the reason why he now lives in one of Waugh's shapeless and meaningless worlds, that of the army. Familiar images of anarchy are associated with it—the temporariness of the army-camp, the lunatic asylum by the gates, the air of grievance and malingering among the men, the performance of meaningless tasks, the uncovering of rubbish to be buried again, the decontamination of an uncontaminated train, the image of encampment in the derelict house. Ryder's actions are meaningless and unredeemed by faith; it is like a bad marriage. "I would go on with my job, but I could bring

G

to it nothing more than acquiescence." He now is virtually on a level with Hooper, "no romantic," and certainly not close to Hooper's opposite, the blustering, bullying commanding officer appealing to standards felt by no one about him. Such a meaningless world it is Waugh's purpose to represent, and then: "My theme is memory, that winged host that soared about me in one grey morning of war-time" he observes, adding that there are few truly vital hours in a lifetime but that these justify existence (like faith), moments of meaning that are the afflatus of the human spirit. Ryder's appreciation of these moments is aesthetic rather than religious, but it constitutes his link with the family whose history, a deep part of his own, he goes on to relate.

This inner action covers a period of just under twenty years beginning shortly after the First World War, when Ryder goes up to Oxford to read History, and ending just before the Second, when he fails to marry Julia. It takes place over a period of great instability in the religious, moral and aesthetic spheres (to all of which due attention is given), a period of personal and social conflict and trauma. The novel is concerned with people falling apart "into separate worlds, little spinning planets of personal relationships," with a civilisation at a stage where "man had deserted his post and the jungle was creeping back to its old strongholds," and with man living with "a small part of [him]self pretending to be whole." Though much of the action takes place among the upper-middle and upper classes (Waugh has said "I reserve the right to deal with the kind of people I know best"[18]) and though the novel takes its standards and attitudes from roughly this *milieu*, there are a great many characters, settings and social classes observed. For Ryder, like so many of Waugh's point-of-view characters, is not himself upper-class or Catholic. He is of an upper-middle-class background; he has lost his mother, and his relations with his father are those of more or less polite warfare; he is an

agnostic and a would-be artist—and the artist is, as
Anthony Blanche ("a nomad of no nationality," "the
aesthete *par excellence*") tells him, "an eternal type, solid,
purposeful, observant." His experience takes him into a
wide society, and his alliance with the Flytes is never
complete. It is marked by doubts, dismissals, warnings
from others; as Anthony Blanche says:

> "It is not an experience I would recommend for An
> Artist at the tenderest stage of his growth, to be
> strangled with charm."[19]

At the beginning of the action he shows conventional
middle-class tastes:

> On my first afternoon [at Oxford] I proudly hung a
> reproduction of Van Gogh's *Sunflowers* over the fire and
> set up a screen, painted by Roger Fry with a Provençal
> landscape, which I had bought inexpensively when the
> Omega workshops were sold up.[20]

and has conventional friends among a small circle of
college intellectuals

> who maintained a middle course of culture between
> the flamboyant "aesthetes" and the proletarian
> scholars who scrambled fiercely for facts in the lodging
> houses of the Iffley Road and Wellington Square.

He chooses not to follow out the usual university career
described to him by his cousin Jasper, but is drawn into
the set around Sebastian Flyte, "entrancing," "with an
epicene beauty which in extreme youth sings aloud for
love and withers at the first cold wind." Flyte stands for
the virtues of unalloyed innocence and youthfulness.
Ryder is tempted but uncertain:

> I went there uncertainly, for it was foreign ground and
> there was a tiny, priggish, warning voice. . . . But I was
> in search of love in those days, and I went full of

curiosity and the faint, unrecognized apprehension that here, at last, I should find that low door in the wall, which others, I knew, had found before me, which opened on an enclosed and enchanted garden. . . .[21]

Here again the paths divide; there is the world of "nursery freshness" and "love" and "a new and secret landscape," represented by Sebastian; and there is the nomad life of the artist, represented by the aesthete Blanche. Either way the life of reason is insufficient— "for the hot spring of anarchy rose from deep furnaces where was no solid earth, and burst into the sunlight . . . with a power the rocks could not repress."[22] He is drawn to an ideal world of innocence, youth, langour and Beatific Vision, a world of the baroque, a world from which man is by his nature an exile, as Sebastian Flyte quickly proves to be. In due course Ryder himself suffers exile for helping Sebastian, but reconciliation to the world of those "hours of afflatus in the human spirit" occurs again when he re-encounters Julia, Sebastian's sister. Both Ryder and she have made unfortunate marriages, to persons of the Hooper world—"I wonder which is the more horrible," I said, "Celia's Art and Fashion or Rex's Politics and Money"[23]—and both, in a scene aboard a Hooper liner, prove themselves by their endurance in a storm to be members of a tough elect (like Mrs Melrose Ape in *Vile Bodies*). They become lovers, agree to marry, and Lord Marchmain even promises them Brideshead, which would be the proper ending to Ryder's search for Arcadia:

> It opened a prospect; the prospect one gained at the turn of the avenue, as I had first seen it with Sebastian, of the secluded valley, the lakes falling away one below the other, the old house in the foreground, the rest of the world abandoned and forgotten; a world of its own of peace and love and beauty; a soldier's dream in a foreign bivouac; such a prospect perhaps as a high

pinnacle of the temple afforded after the hungry days in the desert and the jackal-haunted nights. Need I reproach myself if sometimes I was rapt in the vision?[24]

But other purposes are working themselves out; the world abandoned and forgotten on the one side, and faith abandoned and forgotten on the other, assert their demands; the avalanche descends, destroying and cleansing. Though *Brideshead Revisited* suffers from its lack of conflicts, which makes its plot rather episodic and its tone overly lyrical, it does not (as some critics have supposed) sustain Ryder's myth. His quest is as false as that of any Waugh hero, and success is snatched away as arbitrarily at the last moment. His idea of love has been insufficient; he has, as Blanche says, been strangled with charm; his artistic career and much else have been damaged by that English blight that "spots and kills everything it touches." As in Graham Greene's *The End of the Affair* a higher plotter is at work, using Ryder's story and ambition for His own ends. Ryder, left homeless, childless, middle-aged, loveless, only finds some comfort when he realises the value both of the aspiration and the suffering in some larger action—he sees the flame burning in the *art nouveau* chapel "of deplorable design" at Brideshead, realises it "could not have been but for the builders [of the house] and the tragedians [of the novel]" and ends the book "looking unusually cheerful to-day." Ryder is deprived of the innocent, paradisal world of the beatific vision, symbolised by Brideshead, but through suffering in the incomplete and unsatisfactory adult world he realises his role in the working out of a much more complex process.

Waugh's next work, the story *Scott-King's Modern Europe* (1947), returns to a more comic manner to present a similar problem. An excursion into an area Waugh had long made his own, easily, fluently and very

amusingly presented, this story has a straightforward
plot about a man who leaves a world of retirement in
which he is safe, enters the wild and funny world of
modern politics in an up-to-date, European Azania, and
comes away with the obvious lesson that the modern
world is no place for him—or anyone else, for that
matter. Scott-King is by no means an innocent hero; he
is a worldly-wise man who has made a virtue of detachment. As classics master in a public school he is naturally
on the losing side and accepts the fact:

> he found a peculiar relish in contemplating the
> victories of barbarism and positively rejoiced in his
> reduced station, for he was of a type, unknown in the
> New World, but quite common in Europe, which is
> fascinated by obscurity and failure.[25]

He is nicely poised, wise and wisely obscure, "an adult,
an intellectual . . . travel-worn in the large periphery of
his own mind."[26] But even he is not safe in the world of
have-and-it-shall-be-taken-from-you. Scott-King's weakness is that, being a Mediterranean man, he is filled, when
invited to celebrations commemorating a dim classical poet
of whom he is a scholar, with "deep homesickness for the
south." He accepts the invitation and finds himself in the
wholly absurd, wholly funny totalitarian modern state of
Neutralia, the Bellorius celebration he attends being used
simply as a trick to show Western support for the
incumbent régime. When a political change occurs,
Scott-King is trapped in the country and finally, after
many adventures, escapes, disguised as an Ursuline nun,
to Palestine. On his return he refuses to go along with the
school's policy of fitting boys for the modern world,
describing his refusal as "the most long-sighted view it is
possible to take."[27]

The Loved One: An Anglo-American Tragedy (1948)
shows, in a more extended way, Waugh's remarkable
capacity for seizing on a superb comic opportunity, yet

for seeing the moral and human significance of the absurdity that attracts him; himself a novelist obsessed by death, he could have no better subject than the absurd burial customs of Southern California as they are characterised in the place that Waugh fictionalises into "Whispering Glades." The visitor to Forest Lawn will attest that Waugh has been spared the need to exaggerate. In an article "Death in Hollywood" published in *Life* (29 Sep. 1947) he sketched his response to it by remarking that Dr Eaton, builder of Forest Lawn, "is the first man to offer eternal salvation at an inclusive charge as part of his undertaking service"; he complained too that the traditional concept of death's mystery and enormity were replaced here by an infantile and imbecile idea of the permanence and beauty of life. On its simplest level, the novel is a parody presentation of the artificial, ready-made, simplified life of Southern California, where the falsities of Hollywood are reality and where the absurd chapels ("The Wee Kirk O' Auld Lang Syne") are the truth, are what is. Here Waugh is engaged as a representative of a civilisation with a genuine past, and he shows his English hero's triumphs over the "sparse furniture of [Aimée's] mind." Un-American and un-ethical, drawing on a more complicated response to the world than any of the American (and most of the English) characters, Dennis Barlow has all the advantages of Basil Seal over his environment; he sees the world with greater reality and has the endurance to survive, while those around him, in difficult social or ethical situations, give up, commit suicide. The others live in a world which tastes like Kaiser's Stoneless Peaches, balls of damp, sweet cotton-wool, a world of mechanical expressions, responses, sensations:

Presently he heard steps approach and, without moving, could see that they were a woman's. Feet, ankles, calves came progressively into view. Like every

pair in the country they were slim and neatly covered.
Which came first in this strange civilization, he
wondered, the foot or the shoe, the leg or the nylon
stocking? Or were these uniform elegant limbs, from
the stocking-top down, marketed in one cellophane
envelope at the neighbourhood store? Did they clip by
some labour-saving device to the sterilized rubber
privacies above?[28]

Waugh represents this aspect of American life perfectly,
from Mr Joyboy's Liberace-like "momism" to the details
of the labels on bottles of perfume. But the novel goes
further than that; Dennis Barlow observes that he has
become "the protagonist of a Jamesian problem," a
problem of the encounter of American innocence and
European experience, and points out that James's stories
are "all tragedies one way or another." The international
novel turns on a genuine interpenetration of cultures and
values, and this novel, subtitled *An Anglo-American
Tragedy*, reverses the traditional situation. It is not a
tragedy, of course: the action is another of Waugh's
cruel rituals in a heartless world; it recalls the manner of
the early comedies, save that here Waugh is more deeply
engaged with the ritual's moral significance. Dennis is
one of Waugh's artist-heroes, a young man (one of the
few Waugh heroes not of the author's current age) who
after wingless wartime service in the Royal Air Force has
come to Hollywood to help write a film-life of Shelley.
Reacting against "the monotonous and the makeshift,"
he takes a job as assistant at a pet cemetery, the Happier
Hunting Ground, to the despair of the English colony,
who are keeping up appearances ("they think us cliquey
and stand-offish, but, by God, they respect us"). When
his friend and landlord, an elderly English *literatteur*, is
fired from his studio and commits suicide, Dennis is
involved in a deeper encounter with death. He arranges a
funeral at Whispering Glades and so meets Aimée

Thanatogenos, a cosmetician in the embalming room, an artist in another *genre*. He falls in love with her, but she cannot decide between him and Mr Joyboy, the chief embalmer, who woos her by sending her radiantly smiling corpses. Dennis is sexually pressing, and he sends her poems which his rival, drawing on scholarly help, unmasks as the works of the great romantics. This creates emotional and ethical problems for her, which she solves in the American way by consulting a newspaper advice column in which the Guru Brahmin sets right the difficulties that arise even in this Eden. Unfortunately the Guru Brahmin, a Mr Slump, has just been fired and advises her to jump out of a high window. Instead, she commits suicide in Mr Joyboy's laboratory, causing him to seek Dennis's help in the disposal of this embarrassing extra corpse. The English colony, upset by Dennis's decision to become a non-sectarian clergyman, has just financed his return home; for a consideration from Joyboy which enables him to travel first-class, as he came, he disposes of the body in the Happier Hunting Grounds furnace. Though he has lost Aimée (his loved one now in *both* the senses used in the book), he has acquired the experience he was seeking, and the novel closes on a note of surprising satisfaction:

> On this last evening in Los Angeles Dennis knew he was a favourite of Fortune. Others, better men than he, had foundered here and perished. The strand was littered with their bones. He was leaving it not only unravished but enriched. He was adding his bit to the wreckage; something that had long irked him, his young heart, and was carrying back instead the artist's load, a great, shapeless chunk of experience; bearing it home to his ancient and comfortless shore; to work on it hard and long, for God knew how long. For that moment of vision a lifetime is often too short.

He picked up the novel which Miss Poski had left on

his desk and settled down to await his loved one's final combustion.[29]

The plot, evidently comic in the sense that even the grimmest misfortunes are to Dennis's advantage, turns on a reversal of the traditional tale in which the innocent American comes to Europe for experience. Dennis explores, as it were, the landscape of innocent romanticism; it is in America's innocent Eden, with all its associations with libertarian literature and thought, that Dennis gains his experience. The experience takes him finally, through that romanticism, to a mature art. That Dennis's purpose *is* the pursuit of art is emphasised throughout:

> There was a very long, complicated and important message [the Muse] was trying to convey to him. It was about Whispering Glades, but it was not, except quite indirectly, about Aimée. Sooner or later the Muse would have to be placated. She came first.[30]

A complex literary parody works in the book, and Dennis's quest is in several ways a reversal or mock-version of traditional quests, including that of the romantics for negative capability and for death. His encounter with innocence is in pursuit of experience, and his fascination with Whispering Glades and Aimée is thus defined:

> His interest was no longer purely technical nor purely satiric. Whispering Glades held him in thrall. In that zone of insecurity in the mind where none but the artist dare trespass, the tribes were mustering. . . . There was something in Whispering Glades that was necessary to him, that only he could find.[31]

He is involved in a series of ritual encounters with death, with Aimée and Sir Francis Hindley as unsuccessful fellow-spirits. He tells her:

"we're obsessed by Whispering Glades, both of us—
"half in love with easeful death", as I once told you. . . .
[Y]ou're the nautch girl and vestal virgin of the place,
and naturally I attach myself to you and you attach
yourself to Joyboy. Psychologists will tell you that kind
of thing happens every day. . . ."[32]

But the drowsy numbness and negative capability of
Whispering Glades' Lake Isle of Innisfree (with mechanical bees) quickly fails, for Dennis has a more efficient and
modern idea of death, his strength:

Dennis was a young man of sensibility rather than of
sentiment. He had lived his twenty-eight years at arm's
length from violence, but he came of a generation
which enjoys a vicarious intimacy with death. Never, it
so happened, had he seen a human corpse until that
morning when, returning tired from a night duty, he
found his host strung to the rafters. The spectacle had
been rude and momentarily unnerving; but his reason
accepted the event as part of the established order.[33]

Aimée Thanatogenos ("born of death") becomes the
particular object of his search because of her association
with Whispering Glades, but more because she is out of
the run of identical American women—"sole Eve in a
bustling hygienic Eden, this girl was a decadent . . . her
eyes greenish and remote, with a rich glint of lunacy."
She also retains something of her classical Greek past:

brain and body were scarcely distinguishable from the
standard product, but the spirit—ah, the spirit was
something apart; it had to be sought afar; not here in
the musky orchards of the Hesperides, but in the
mountain air of the dawn, in the eagle-haunted passes
of Hellas.

In her death she communes with the spirit of her ancestors,
"the impious and haunted race," and the deity she

serves; the death is presented as something beyond the
ethical tension that seems to provoke it. Like Dennis a
decadent and an exile in Eden, she reverts, dying, to the
pagan stoicism of her ancestors, becomes Alcestis or
Helen. It is more than irony that she should be incinerated
not at Whispering Glades but at the animal cemetery.
Throughout the book the Happier Hunting Ground has
been a parody of the greater institution ("Dog that is
born of bitch hath but a short time to live, and is full of
misery . . ."), the only effective parody in the circumstances; and it is associated with the lesson of human
animality which is so much a part of Waugh's comic
view. Thus Aimée's death is an appropriate ritual, and
has its parody festivities. Dennis reads one of the parody
poems ("Aimée, thy beauty is to me . . ."), indicating
that Aimée is a Helen, undergoing some classical ritual in
keeping with her reversion to her ancestors. She has been
at once Dennis's guide through the underworld and the
victim of his power to survive her; like Sir Francis, she is
a *memento mori*, but also his guide on the journey through
romanticism to classicism, through America back to his
native shore. *The Loved One* is Christian satire[34] but it is
also classical in its myth. Dennis learns not because
Aimée suffers but because, like Dante's Virgil, she leads.

Dennis's almost successful quest, which takes him
beyond his Helen to his own native shore, ancient and
comfortless, takes its shape from comic necessity; the
successful quest of Helena, the hero of Waugh's next
novel, is however historically decided. *Helena* (1950) is of
all Waugh's novels the most difficult for the non-Catholic
reader to respond to, for Helena exists in a special order
of sanctity. Though the preface tells us that the book
("just something to read; in fact a legend") interprets its
traditional and historical materials with a novelist's
preference for the picturesque over the plausible, it is a
novel about faith, Helena being created for a particular
task, one of sainthood, and aided by a dream indicating

divine intervention. Since Helena's success is foreknown, our attention necessarily turns to more incidental aspects of presentation—the excellent social analysis, the remarkable evocation of the life of Constantine's Rome, the ironic references to present-day conditions—and, particularly, to the very explicit delineation of the tolerant, eclectic vein in Waugh's Catholic thought, to which insufficient attention is usually paid. The novel is concerned with the consequences of Catholicism for present-day Europe, with the growth of business and politics that accompanied the rise of the faith, with the various perversities that faith can contain. Constantine, Helena's son, absurd yet tragic in his green wig, "Power without Grace," prefigures the world of political democracy in which all men take on power without divine support. A further theme in the novel, one of the series which Waugh intended showing the relation between England and the Holy Places,[35] is the contest between British common sense and eastern mysticism; it is not only Helena but her prosaic, a-political culture that enjoys the triumph of the discovery of the Cross. The opening paragraph suggests that Waugh's aim is comically anti-romantic:

> Once, very long ago, before ever the flowers were named which struggled and fluttered below the rain-swept walls, there sat at an upper window a princess and a slave reading a story which even then was old: or rather, to be entirely prosaic, on the wet afternoon of the Nones of May in the year (as it was computed later) of Our Lord 273, in the city of Colchester, Helena, red-haired, youngest daughter of the Coel, Paramount Chief of the Trinovantes, gazed into the rain while her tutor read the Iliad of Homer in a Latin paraphrase.[36]

This vein of comedy is, in the early chapters, rather whimsical and arch. Helena is drawn as a rather sexless,

Brenda Last-ish, twentieth-century schoolgirl in a society of aristocrats and soldiers; her father King Coel (equipped with pipe, bowl and fiddlers) is an old Waugh type—he warns her that the Roman Constantius who wants to marry her is a "relation of the Divine What-d'you-call-him—awful fellow who was Emperor not long ago. Says he comes from the Balkans somewhere."[37] The young Helena has the "heroic myths" of other Waugh heroes, which she regards with a mixture of awe and "homely humorous intimacy"; she is inspired by the ideal of the City, half Rome, half buried Troy. As a young girl she wants to travel and quest, to find out what lies beyond the bounds of civilisation, and rejects Constantius's notion of the wall of empire, which has "inside, peace, decency, the law, the altars of the Gods, industry, the arts, order; outside, wild beasts and savages, forest and swamp, bloody mumbo-jumbo, men like wolf-packs." She wants an undivided world, with the wall at its limits, so that all may share the City. This ideal continues after her conversion as a notion of an eclectic, a catholic faith.

"Odi profanum vulgus et arceo." That was an echo from the old empty world. There was no hate in her now and nothing round her was quite profane. . . . There was no mob, only a vast multitude of souls, clothed in a vast variety of body, milling about in the Holy City, in the See of Peter.[38]

Constantine's ambition is political, for the great earthly city; that, like the idea of the Holy City whose walls "shut out all the evil passions of the world," is false, and Helena turns to the possibility of reconciling all differences, pretensions, falsities and subtleties by guiding the Faith toward Reasonableness through the discovery of the True Cross, symbol of God's purposefulness: .

"Just at this moment when everyone is forgetting [the

Cross] and chattering about the hypostatic union, there's a solid chunk of wood waiting for them to have their silly heads knocked against. I'm going off to find it."[39]

Guided in a dream by the Wandering Jew, who for commercial purposes wants her to succeed, she finds the Cross and so provides a truthful centre for the variousness of the Faith. The Cross "states a fact" and Helena's cry of "bosh" to all those who have fanciful theories about Cross or Faith explains her plain British characterisation: but thus she creates a faith that can contain "the learned, the oblique, the delicate" as well as the simple. Donat O'Donnell's description of the book as "a shapeless, sentimental novel about the piety of a British lady in the age of Constantine, epoch of the conversion of the upper classes"[40] is unfair; the stress falls on the openness, reasonableness and universality of the Church, and the book is a significant document for Waugh's own kind of faith and indeed for his problems as a comic novelist, writing novels that, while not usually depictions of a God-governed universe, represent the "wild beasts and savages" which faith must include. This historical romance is idiosyncratic and allows no real room for his best powers, but it is an important indication both of his varied technical resources and his way of using his faith and opinions in fiction.

The success or failure of Waugh's later books seems to depend on the degree to which he is prepared to "go native," as Dennis Barlow did, to follow the demands of the imagination unresistingly into a barbarian world. *Love Among the Ruins: A Romance of the Near Future* (1953), an anti-Utopian macabre comedy projected forward into a *1984* world of totalitarianism, rehabilitation centres, Departments of Euthanasia and the like, rather lacks the required liveliness; while the plot offers a "hopeful" picture of anarchy in man, it is not instinctively and

comically engaged with it. Miles Plastic, the hero, is an
arsonist who rebels against life in Institutions, which here
create man, deny human responsibility, debilitate individual existence ("This little pile of papers is *You*"), and
promote the death-wish. Miles is influenced by Mountjoy,
a stately home adapted into the centre where he is
"rehabilitated," into becoming a decadent in love with
the past. He has an affair, charmingly presented, with
Clara, a ballet-dancer who has grown a beard as a result
of a botched sterilisation operation. When she aborts her
child by Miles and has her beard removed by plastic
surgery, he burns down Mountjoy, trophy of a fading
dream, and returns to the fold. Mountjoy is replaced by a
new packing-case building, Miles makes a convenient
marriage, "Modern Man was home." Or almost: for,
with Waugh's evident approval, the unregenerate spirit
reappears when at his wedding Miles feels a cigarette
lighter in his pocket and presses it—"instantly, sur-
prisingly there burst out a tiny flame—gemlike, hymeneal,
auspicious."

A much better book is *The Ordeal of Gilbert Pinfold*
(1957), a frankly confessional "conversation piece" and
study in hallucination. Pinfold is sympathetically presented, but by an omniscient narrator "above" him, with
access to his mind and impressions but also to the reality
which he gradually leaves behind. This approach allows
Pinfold's values to be offered with a faint irony, and
more importantly for the weaknesses in his situation in
the opening to be exposed and challenged. He is then a
contented man, "unusually free from the fashionable
agonies of *angst*," but with several flaws—distrustful of
others, fearful of attacks on his modesty, he has built up
an elaborate defensive facade; he is bored and emotionally
discontented after having abandoned the "amusements"
of his youth; he upholds an old-fashioned romantic
patriotism; he suffers from insomnia. He takes medicines
to alleviate his insomnia and boredom; these affect his

memory and increase his paranoia, loosening his grip on
reality. For curative purposes he sails on the *S.S. Caliban*
—Master, Captain Steerforth—for Ceylon, and the
nether-world of his own mind. Hallucinations begin; he
seems to hear through the ship's pipes a band, a nonconformist service, a mutiny, things disturbing and
offensive to him. Gradually the voices turn against him; a
radio broadcast seems to attack his fiction for "cloying
religiosity"; other "passengers" accuse him of being a
Jew, a Communist, a sodomite, a new man of the Tudor
period, an exploiting landowner, a cruel son. The
charges, though inconsistent within themselves, have a
savage accuracy, being a corrupt version of his own self-
image. They possess something of the remote, improbable
logic Waugh sets up in his comedy when the control of
orderly behaviour is released, and a new and farcical set
of rules appears under the impulse of some imaginative
principle which, like Graves-Upton's mysterious box,
"only transmits *Life* Forces." They are meaningful and
dangerous, for they have qualities of vision, to which
Pinfold is receptive; they are a genuine mystery.

As he overhears people talking about him in what he at
first thinks to be a cruel game of persecution, Pinfold's
behaviour grows more eccentric. The hoaxes grow in
complexity, for Pinfold seems to make discoveries about
his persecutors and then finds those to be hoaxes too. His
patriotism and his sexuality are probed; a voice named
Margaret falls in love with him and promises to visit his
cabin, provoking a moral and religious crisis about his
marriage but ending with his willingness to meet "love."
Finally Pinfold seems to see "the heart of the mystery"—
the voices become concentrated in Margaret his "lover"
and a Machievellian B.B.C. man named Angel who is
compiling a dossier on him, charting his state of consciousness and trying to psycho-analyse him with an
elaborate radio equipment. The hallucination has been
able to survive through Margaret's "Rules" ("it's a Rule

that no one else must be told") but Pinfold finally writes home to his wife:

> *They first break the patient's nerve by all sorts of violent scenes which he thinks are really happening. . . . I'm not the first person they tried it on. They drove an actor to suicide . . .*

He also has a more important insight: "*Sometimes I wonder whether it is not literally the Devil who is molesting me.*" His wife rescues him by forcing him to come home; he returns to ordinary reality, knowing that he has "endured a great ordeal and, unaided, had emerged the victor." Only by confession and communication has he been saved; the force and seriousness of the last pages come from his conviction that if he had kept the Rules the voices would never have left him. Through the "sheer bad temper" which has made him confess, reason and modesty have triumphed over a dangerous power: "There was a triumph to be celebrated, even if a mocking slave stood always beside him in his chariot reminding him of mortality." The final act of confession and distancing comes when Pinfold sits down to transpose the material into art.

The three novels forming the *Men at Arms* trilogy, written over this same period, have a similar confessional quality, a similar irony. They form a remarkable war-novel, surely the most important novel about the Second World War to appear in England, and treat ironically the notion of the just war, showing that war not as an epic action but as a succession of absurd or ignomious episodes, cruel excesses, mistaken alliances. The main events are concerned with an historical happening, the War, to which the hero Guy Crouchback attempts to attach his destiny; and this hero, close to Waugh, undergoes an ordeal or search in which his own values are threatened and finally changed, and with whom the reader is involved in a complex relationship of sympathy and distrust. Since Waugh is seeking to deal in detail

with the nature and meaning of a modern historical
event, the novels are slow-paced, given up to incidental
episodes and much historical detail, and since his
approach is that of deflation they depend for many of
their effects on scenes of buffoonery and farce, and
extended comic set-pieces, like the episode of Apthorpe's
Thunder-Box. Closer to the conventional socio-comic
novel, to Powell or Amis, than anything else of Waugh's,
they contain some of his funniest, most graceful and most
devastating writing. Guy's false quest is super-imposed on
this loosely-drawn narrative line, and gives meaning to
the action, a meaning won from the chaos, the arbitrary
movement of men in incomprehensible actions, mysterious
troop-movements, aimless commands. A mass of different
characters appears, all playing their small parts in this
chaotic world, and one theme in the novel is the search
for meaning amid the welter of event, in which death,
disaster and disappearance are commonplace, character
is fluid, men constantly violate the rules they are expected
to follow, for good ends and bad. Apparent systems of
order, those of class, duty or faith, contrast with the flux;
stable places, Broome, Bellamy's, the Halberdiers Mess,
contrast with places of disorder, like the military encamp-
ments in Capetown, Crete, Alexandria, Yugoslavia. War
emphasises uncertainty and double-dealing, for it is full
of various codes and causes, strange alliances of interest,
curious meetings of men. In this uncertainty those who
manage best are those without character or identity,
people like Ludovic or Kilbannock who can speak the
language of all classes, be both masters and men. Thus,
commitment to a belief becomes a kind of impersonation,
and Guy feels that "his whole uniform was a disguise, his
whole calling a masquerade"; a sense of the oddity of
real character dominates the book, adding force to its
concern with faithlessness and betrayal. The duties and
obligations under which men serve invite pretence and
treachery; the action abounds with spies, traitors,

cowards, people in positions of ironic duty, like the Communists in H.O.O. Headquarters and Trimmer in his role as hero. Much of the farce comes out of such absurdities. In war, a strange variety of men come together on what is supposedly a common mission, but for most of them it simply satisfies personal, political or financial ambitions (Waugh has long had this view of warfare, and the end of *Put Out More Flags* seems little more than a gesture to unity). Their final lack of dedication is revealed by comparison with the central character; Guy is distinguished by wishing the War to be a clearcut cause. He has, indeed, epic ambitions.

Guy's role is defined according to certain historical and mythical patterns that shape the direction of his quest. A Catholic, the last of a line of depressed landed aristocrats and soldiers of recusant history, he possesses a romantic ideal of military service; to be a soldier in a just war is both a crusade and a pilgrimage, and he at first sees the War as "a time of glory and dedication." His ideal of defending country and faith is formed half by the storybooks he has read as a boy, particularly on the adventures of a Captain Truslove, and half by the military crusades, typified for him by Roger de Waybroke, whose tomb in the Italian village where Guy lived before the War shows where his crusade was broken. He thus regards the War as one of justice and faith demanding common cause on his own side and the unconditional surrender of the enemy. The Russo-German alliance means that for him the battle can be a crusade against all that is wrong in the world:

> The enemy at last was plain in view, huge and hateful, all disguise cast off. It was the Modern Age in arms. Whatever the outcome there was a place for him in that battle.

But Guy's own way is already broken. He is in a dark wood in the middle of life's journey, looking for a guide and mentor to lead him to redemption. He is thirty-five when the story opens, and in a state of spiritual and emotional aridity:

> It was as though eight years back [when he had divorced his wife] he had suffered a tiny stroke of paralysis; all his spiritual faculties were just perceptibly impaired.

Without a full personal reality, a feather in a vacuum, he lives through the three novels in a state of spiritual apathy in which he is unable to ask anything of God. He has his seasons of hope and of despair: all three books begin in light spirit with a series of events in training, set in England, with Guy's mood a hopeful one, and all conclude with events in action abroad, where Guy witnesses and is involved in a betrayal, as a result of which he suffers in reputation, hope and faith. Thus he passes through a series of stages in a spiritual experience, enacted in a mock-Dantean underworld, presented often in comic terms. He clearly does regard the world as a testing place, part of the supernatural order:

> "Do you agree," he asked earnestly, "that the Supernatural Order is not something added to the Natural Order, like music or painting, to make everyday life more tolerable? It *is* real life. The supernatural is real; what we call 'real' is a mere shadow, a passing fancy."[41]

Waugh also refers to the Troy story, with its quest for the lost city and the lost queen of love: Guy's former wife, whom he remarries is named Virginia Troy ("Like Helen of Troy," says Guy) and again the Mediterranean appears as the great centre of life and feeling, source of faith and love, where his forebears have found happiness and exultation. It is to a much modified version of that buried city, the "Lesser House," that Guy finally comes, tired and late.

Guy's progress through the War is thus half epic pilgrimage, half a comic game of spiritual snakes and ladders. In *Men at Arms* (1952) Guy sets out to follow Sir Roger de Waybroke, but instead becomes involved with his farcical *alter ego*, Apthorpe, for whose death he bears some responsibility. In *Officers and Gentlemen* (1955) he realises that "an act of *pietas* was required of him" and conveys Apthorpe's belongings to his friend "Chatty" Corner, who lives in a "dark tower" on the Isle of Mugg. The handing over is a "holy moment"; Apthorpe's shade is placated, Guy is recalled to the life of action. In this book he finds a new *alter ego*, Ivor Claire, an aesthete who deserts his men in Crete, and who betrays the code of upper-class honour to which he belongs. In *Unconditional Surrender* (1961) a new *alter ego* emerges in the complex figure of Ludovic, who has killed Major "Fido" Hound and an unnamed sapper in the retreat in Crete and fears that Guy knows this. Ludovic is "like the Angel of Death," and is described by another character as a Zombie—"Men who are dug up and put to work and then buried again." He is a writer, a classless man, a keeper of a strange journal ("Major Hound seems strangely lacking in the Death-Wish"), who wants Guy's death, and is a figure for that death-wish that a "celebrated English composer" discerns in Guy, and which he confesses to a priest as presumption ("I am not fit to die"). If Claire stands too for the decline of the upper class "Bloods" with whom Guy began the War, and who meet together in the Commandos, Ludovic represents the spirit of the latter days of the War, when the common cause with the Russians has turned it into a People's War; his purchase of Guy's Italian castle is a significant moment of supersession. *Unconditional Surrender* is in fact a novel of deaths, wished and unwished, those of Guy's father, his wife and his old hero Ritchie-Hook (in the earlier part of the action a kind of Grimesian life-force) being the most significant. Guy does survive, changed in mind and situation, his pilgrimage unfinished, his crusade regretted, in the Lesser House on his family estate at Broome. But he marries again, bringing up Trimmer's child as his heir, a final act of *pietas*.

The main themes of the Crouchback narrative deal, then with Guy's attitude toward the dry and empty parts of his own character, seen in emotional and spiritual terms; with his attitude towards his heritage as a Catholic and an aristocrat; and with his attitude towards his society, its political schisms and changes, and the war that comes out of those schisms and in fact does nothing to change them. In some sense all these problems are solved by two acts of compassion, Guy's remarriage to Virginia, with her "faint, indelible signature of failure, degradation and despair," and his taking responsibility for her child by Trimmer; and his sympathetic, guilty action on behalf of the Jews who are left uncared for by the Yugoslav partisans. Guy inherits a lesson from his father:

> The Mystical Body doesn't strike attitudes or stand on its dignity. It accepts suffering and injustice. . . . Quantitative judgments don't apply.

The novel has begun with hope for Guy's crusade; when he joins the Halberdiers, a corps with distinctive traditions and high standards of conduct, and finds that he is fighting the War with men who seem to share some of his convictions, he has grounds for hope, though disillusionments come rapidly. The Commandos, in which the young "bloods" of Bellamy's are fighting the War with their friends, offers a second moment of hope, ended with Clare's treachery and his supersession by Ludovic. But *Unconditional Surrender* is dominated by the image of the mismade and misbegotten sword of Stalingrad, the symbol of the People's War, and of the reassertion of schism, politics and cruelty, and Guy must build his hope on a Lesser House. The point is put to him by one of the

Jews after Guy has imagined himself as a Moses leading them from bondage.

> "Is there any place that is free from evil? It is too simple to say that only the Nazis wanted war. These communists wanted it too. It was the only way in which they could come to power. Many of my people wanted it, to be revenged on the Germans, to hasten the creation of the national state. It seems to me there was a will to war, a death wish, everywhere. Even good men thought their private honour could be satisfied by war. They could assert their manhood by killing and being killed. They would accept hardships in recompense from being selfish and lazy. Danger justified privilege. I knew Italians—not very many perhaps—who felt this. Were there none in England?"

"God forgive me," said Guy, "I was one of them."[42]

Guy thus comes to terms with the Modern Age in Arms, and a new age begins with his understanding. He does not like the People's War or the People's Peace, but he is reconciled by the compassion he has felt as well as by his sense of futility in the face of those who feel that the War is ending with justice being done. His unconditional surrender is to God as well as to the pressing world, and this involves the recognition that God's will has not been as simple as he has supposed. In *Men at Arms* Guy meets Mr Goodall, an ex-teacher who sees providence at work in the history of the Catholic recusant families. Guy asks him whether he seriously believes "that God's Providence concerns itself with the perpetuation of the English Catholic aristocracy." "But of course. And with sparrows, too, we are taught." God is not enlisted on the side of the just cause but enables justice to come indirectly out of the events, even if it is only the salvation of a single soul.

The sense of the mystery of Providence is kept alive throughout the books. They are full of strange interventions on Guy's behalf or against him, and characters in the background play their remote roles in his destiny with the same sort of perseverance as do the Angels in *Gilbert Pinfold*. Two of the main figures who influence his life are an unknown major, who helps him frequently, reappearing from place to place, and the mysterious secret service man Grace-Groundling-Marchpole, who keeps a file on him and stops his promotion; at the end of *Unconditional Surrender* these are revealed to be brothers—a "special aura always attaches . . . to those figures . . . who facilitate the hero's movement in a strange world, and enable him to achieve his ambition."[43] The roles played by the other characters and by the events in the action are given enormous relevance to Guy's blundering journey. Each novel forms a distinctive experience, dominated by certain themes, certain characters, a certain social, moral and spiritual atmosphere. *Men at Arms* is, socially, upper- and upper-middle-class; its main theme is education and the taking on of roles; its spiritual concern is with the search for identity. *Officers and Gentlemen*, showing the decline of traditional values, presents the supersession of the upper-class heroes, the "fine flower of the nation," by the people's "heroes," Trimmer and Ludovic; its theme is retreat and suffering; in its spiritual dimension it is concerned with the search for a cause. *Unconditional Surrender* takes place largely in a people's world, the supersession of the upper class having been virtually completed; its theme is that of finding life in death, and spiritually it is concerned with the growth of compassion. While Guy "leads" the action in each of these books, he is placed in relation to it, limited by it. We see him from many points of view. Virginia describes him as a "wet, smug, obscene, pompous, sexless lunatic pig," and Apthorpe represents a higher version of his comic absurdity. He is through most of the action a comic cuckold, and he is significantly weak in the legs (most of the upper-class characters undergo sprained knees or broken legs). The action extends beyond him

and places him, leading him into mystification. Like
Sir Roger de Waybroke and like his own forebears he
never really meets the enemy, be it either the Germans
or within his own camp:

> In this limbo Guy fretted for more than a week
> while February blossomed into March. He had left
> Italy four and a half years ago. He had then taken
> leave of the crusader whom the people called "il santo
> inglese". He had laid his hand on the sword which had
> never struck the infidel. He wore the medal which had
> hung round the neck of his brother, Gervase, when the
> sniper had picked him off on his way up to the line in
> Flanders. In his heart he felt stirring the despair in
> which his brother, Ivo, had starved himself to death.
> Half an hour's scramble on the beach near Dakar; an
> ignominious rout in Crete. That had been his war.[44]

If, then, at the end of the novel things have "turned out
very conveniently for Guy" it is only in a limited and
ironical way, a way which has involved his unconditional
surrender. As at the end of *Howards End*, the son who is
to inherit mixes the classes. In this sense he may be a
symbol of Guy's failure, but the very continuance of the
line, for which Guy as heir is responsible, is ensured by
the same fact. The young Trimmer is one of Waugh's
deepest ironies, and implies the deflation of the myth that
Donat O'Donnell finds in *Brideshead Revisited*. Guy comes
to terms with the surrounding anarchy at the expense of
his myth, and the "high-romantic" features that Philip
Toynbee finds in the trilogy[45] are in fact much modified
by the ending. The trilogy, so complicated in its presentation, so varied in its tone, is among Waugh's best work,
and brings together the realistic and farcical elements
always present to different degrees in a happy relationship, making use of all his best technical resources. As in
all Waugh's later work, his positive respect for the serious,
the traditional and the Catholic grows more and more

clear, and the idea of the heroic Christian gentleman emerges. What is always shown, however, is his failure; the other world, the world of anarchy and disorder, remains, and is never finally brought under control. In this respect Waugh is a totally modern novelist, offering his own values with assertive prejudice, but in a world where the really truthful statement is that of flux and anarchy.

REFERENCES

1. "Fan-Fare," 1946, p. 56.
2. *W.S.*, p. 239.
3. *W.S.*, p. 190.
4. *W.S.*, p. 145.
5. *W.S.*, pp. 212–13.
6. *W.S.*, p. 222.
7. *P.M.F.*, p. 11.
8. *P.M.F.*, pp. 34–5.
9. *P.M.F.*, p. 230.
10. *P.M.F.*, p. 220.
11. "Preface," *B.R.* (Revised edn.).
12. Rose Macaulay, "Evelyn Waugh," 1948, p. 147.
13. Donat O'Donnell, *Maria Cross*, 1952, pp. 119–34.
14. Frank Kermode, "Mr. Waugh's Cities," 1962, p. 174.
15. "Preface," *B.R.* (Revised edn.).
16. David Lodge, *Catholic Fiction since the Oxford Movement*, pp. 585–649.
17. *B.R.*, p. 304.
18. "Fan-Fare," 1946, p. 60.
19. *B.R.*, p. 52.
20. *B.R.*, pp. 25–26.
21. *B.R.*, p. 29.
22. *B.R.*, p. 41.
23. *B.R.*, p. 242.
24. *B.R.*, p. 282.
25. *Scott-King's Modern Europe*, pp. 2–3.
26. *Op. cit.*, p. 9.
27. *Op. cit.*, p. 88.
28. *L.O.*, p. 74.
29. *L.O.*, pp. 143–4.
30. *L.O.*, p. 90.
31. *L.O.*, pp. 68–9.
32. *L.O.*, p. 124.
33. *L.O.*, p. 31.
34. Cp. David Lodge, *op. cit.*
35. Cp. p. 28 above.
36. *H.*, p. 1.
37. *H.*, p. 32.
38. *H.*, pp. 145–6.
39. *H.*, p. 209.
40. Donat O'Donnell, *op. cit.*, p. 134.
41. *M.A.*, p. 89.
42. *U.S.*, p. 300.
43. Stopp, p. 167.
44. *U.S.*, p. 217.
45. Philip Toynbee, "Evelyn Waugh: Mourner for a World that Never Was," 1961, p. 21.

SELECT BIBLIOGRAPHY

Note

The following select bibliography is based largely on Paul A. Doyle's excellent "Evelyn Waugh: A Bibliography (1926–1956)" in *Bulletin of Bibliography* (Boston, U.S.A.), xxii, 3 (May–Aug. 1957), pp. 57 ff. It should be noted that Waugh sometimes changes the titles and occasionally even the text of the American versions of his novels, stories, travel-books and essays, and often publishes articles, etc. several times.

References in the text are to editions marked * in this bibliography. Chapman and Hall have published a uniform edition of the novels up to and including *Brideshead Revisited*. My practice has been to refer to this where extant (except where Waugh has revised the text, in which cases comparative references have been made). Waugh is currently engaged in revising some of his novels and revised editions already published are indicated by R.E. Small revisions of his work appear *passim*.

I. EVELYN WAUGH

1. Novels and Collected Short Stories

Decline and Fall: An Illustrated Novelette. London (Chapman and Hall) 1928. New York (Farrar and Rinehart) 1929. *Uniform edn. 1947. *R. E. (Chapman and Hall) 1962. Penguin Books, 1937.

Vile Bodies. London (Chapman and Hall) and New York (J. Cape and H. Smith) 1930. *Uniform edn. 1947. Penguin Books, 1938.

Black Mischief. London (Chapman and Hall) and New York (Farrar and Rinehart) 1932. *Uniform edn. 1948. Penguin Books, 1938.

A Handful of Dust. London (Chapman and Hall) and New York (Farrar and Rinehart) 1934. *Uniform edn. 1948. Penguin Books, 1951.

Mr. Loveday's Little Outing, and Other Sad Stories. *London (Chapman and Hall) and Boston (Little, Brown) 1936. (Many of these stories were reprinted in *Work Suspended*, listed below.)

Scoop: A Novel About Journalists. London (Chapman and Hall); Boston (Little, Brown) and Toronto (Ryerson Press) 1938. *Uniform edn. 1948. Penguin Books, 1944.

Put Out More Flags. London (Chapman and Hall) and Boston (Little, Brown) 1942. *Uniform edn. 1948. Penguin Books, 1943.

Work Suspended. London (Chapman and Hall) 1942. Reprinted in amended form in *Work Suspended, and Other Stories Written Before* *the Second World War*, *Uniform edn. 1949. (This contains a number of stories from *Mr. Loveday's Little Outing*.) *W.S.* appears in the U.S.A. as part of *Tactical Exercise*, listed below. Penguin Books, 1951 (with *Scott-King's Modern Europe*, *et al.*).

Brideshead Revisited: The Sacred and Profane Memories of Captain Charles Ryder. London (Chapman and Hall); Boston (Little, Brown) and Toronto (Ryerson Press) 1945. *Uniform edn. 1949. *R.E. (Chapman and Hall) 1960. Penguin Books, 1951.

Scott-King's Modern Europe. *London (Chapman and Hall) 1947. Boston (Little, Brown) 1949. Penguin Books, 1951 (with *W.S.*, *et al.*).

The Loved One: An Anglo-American Tragedy. *London (Chapman and Hall); Boston (Little, Brown) and Toronto (Smithers and Bonellie) 1948. Penguin Books, 1951.

Helena. London (Chapman and Hall) and Boston (Little, Brown) 1950. *Uniform edn. 1957. Penguin Books, 1963.

Men at Arms. *London (Chapman and Hall) and Boston (Little, Brown) 1952. (First of a trilogy.)

Love Among the Ruins: A Romance of the Near Future. *London (Chapman and Hall) 1953. Printed in the U.S.A. as part of *Tactical Exercise*, listed below. Penguin Books, 1963 (with *O.G.P.* and *Tactical Exercise*.)

Tactical Exercise. Boston (Little, Brown) 1954. (Contains *W.S.*, *L.A.R.*, *et al.*).

Officers and Gentlemen. *London (Chapman and Hall) and Boston (Little, Brown) 1955. (Second of a trilogy.)

The Ordeal of Gilbert Pinfold: A Conversation Piece. *London (Chapman and Hall) and *Boston (Little, Brown) 1957. Penguin Books, 1963 (with *L.A.R.*, *et al.*).

Unconditional Surrender: the Conclusion of "Men at Arms" and "Officers and Gentlemen". *London (Chapman and Hall) 1961. Entitled *The End of the Battle*, Boston (Little, Brown) 1962.

2. Travel Books, Biography, Criticism

Rossetti: His Life and Works. *London (Duckworth) and New York (Dodd, Mead and Co.) 1928.

Labels: A Mediterranean Journal. *London (Duckworth) 1930. Entitled *A Bachelor Abroad: A Mediterranean Journal*, New York (J. Cape and H. Smith) 1930. (Parts of *L.* reprinted in *W.G.G.*, listed below.)

Remote People. *London (Duckworth) 1931. Entitled *They Were Still Dancing*, New York (Farrar and Rinehart) 1932. (Parts of *R.P.* reprinted in *W.G.G.*)

Ninety-Two Days: the account of a tropical journey through British Guiana and part of Brazil. *London (Duckworth) 1934. New

York (Farrar and Rinehart) 1934. (Parts of *N.—T.D.* reprinted in *W.G.G.*).

Edmund Campion. *London (Sheed and Ward) and Toronto (Longmans Green and Co.) 1935. Boston, Little, Brown, 1946. *R.E., 1947. Penguin Books, 1953.

Waugh in Abyssinia. *London and New York (Longmans Green and Co.) 1936. (Parts of *W.A.* reprinted in *W.G.G.*).

Robbery Under Law: The Mexican Object-lesson. *London (Chapman and Hall) 1939. Entitled *Mexico: an object-lesson*, Boston (Little, Brown) 1939.

When the Going Was Good. (Selections from earlier travel books, with introduction.) *London (Duckworth) and Toronto (Thomas Nelson and Sons) 1946. Boston (Little, Brown) 1947. Penguin Books, 1951.

The Holy Places. (Three essays.) *London (The Queen Anne Press) 1952 (limited edn.).

The Life of the Right Reverend Ronald Knox, Fellow of Trinity College Oxford, and Pronotary Apostolic to His Holiness Pope Pius XII. *London (Chapman and Hall); Boston (Little, Brown) and Toronto (Ryerson Press) 1959. Fontana Books, 1962.

A Tourist in Africa. *London (Chapman and Hall); Boston (Little, Brown) and Toronto (Ryerson Press) 1960.

3. Miscellaneous Articles

"Dante Gabriel Rossetti: a centenary criticism," in *Fortnightly Review*, n.s., CXXIX (1928), pp. 595–604.

"Ronald Firbank," in *Life and Letters*, II (1929), pp. 570–1.

"Authors Take Sides on the Spanish War," in *Left Review*, (1937).

"Commando Raid on Bardia," in *Life*, XI (1941), pp. 63–6, 71, 72, 74.

"Fan-Fare," in *Life*, XX (1946), pp. 53, 54, 56, 58, 60.

"Death in Hollywood." in *Life*, XXIII (1947), pp. 73–4, 79–80, 83–4.

"Mgr. Ronald Knox," in *Horizon*, XVII (1948), pp. 326–38.

"Come Inside," in *The Road to Damascus*, ed. John A. O'Brien, London 1949, VOL. I, pp. 10–16.

"Max Beerbohm, a lesson in manners," in *The Atlantic*, CXCVIII (1956), pp. 75–6.

"An open letter to the Honourable Mrs. Peter Rodd (Nancy Mitford) on a Very Serious Subject," in *Noblesse Oblige: An Enquiry into the Identifiable Characteristics of the English Aristocracy.* London 1956, pp. 65–82.

"An Act of Homage and Reparation to P. G. Wodehouse," in *The Sunday Times*, No. 7209 (16 July, 1961), pp. 21, 23.

"My Father," in *The Sunday Telegraph*, No. 96 (2 Dec. 1962), pp. 4, 5.

II. OTHERS

1. Biographical

ACTON, HAROLD: *Memoirs of an Aesthete*, London 1948.

BALFOUR, PATRICK (Lord Kinross): *Society Racket: A Critical Account of Modern Social Life*, London n.d. [1933].

BIRKENHEAD, LORD: *Lady Eleanor Smith, A Memoir*, London 1953.

CAREW, DUDLEY: *The House Is Gone, A Personal Retrospect*. London n.d. [1949].

PAKENHAM, LORD: *Born to Believe*, London 1953.

SAUNDERS, H. ST GEORGE: *The Green Beret, The Story of the Commandos 1940–5*, London 1949.

WAUGH, ALEC: *The Early Years of Alec Waugh*, London 1962.

WAUGH, ARTHUR: *One Man's Road*, London 1931.

2. Critical

BERGONZI, BERNARD: "Evelyn Waugh's Gentleman," in *Critical Quarterly*, v, 1963, pp. 23–36.

DENNIS, NIGEL: "Evelyn Waugh: The Pillar of Anchorage House," in *Partisan Review* (New York), x, 1943, pp. 350–61.

DEVITIS, A. A.: *Roman Holiday: The Catholic Novels of Evelyn Waugh*. New York 1956.

DOYLE, PAUL A.: "The Politics of Waugh," in *Renascence*, XI, 1959, pp. 171–74, 221.

DYSON, A. E.: "Evelyn Waugh and the Mysteriously Disappearing Hero," in *Critical Quarterly*, II, 1960, pp. 72–9.

GORE ALLEN, W.: "Evelyn Waugh and Graham Greene," in *Irish Monthly*, LXXVII, 1949, pp. 16–22.

GRACE, WILLIAM J.: "Evelyn Waugh as a Social Critic," in *Renascence*, I, 1949, pp. 28–40.

GREEN, MARTIN: "British Comedy and the British Sense of Humour: Shaw, Waugh, and Amis." in *The Texas Quarterly*, IV, 1961, pp. 217–27; and "Meaning and Delight in Evelyn Waugh" (unpublished article).

GREEN, PETER: "Du Côté de Chez Waugh," in *Review of English Literature*, II, 1961, pp. 89–100.

GRIFFITHS, JOAN: "Waugh's Problem Comedies," in *Accent*, IX, 1949, pp. 165–70.

HALL, JAMES: "The Other Post-War Rebellion: Evelyn Waugh Twenty-Five Years After," in *E.L.H.*, XXVIII, 1961, pp. 187–202.

HEILMAN, ROBERT B.: "Sue Bridehead Revisited," in *Accent*, VII, 1947, pp. 123–26.

HIGHET, GILBERT: *The Art of Satire*, Princeton/Oxford 1962.

HOLLIS, CHRISTOPHER: *Evelyn Waugh*, London 1954 (R.E., 1958).

KERMODE, FRANK: "Mr. Waugh's Cities," in *Puzzles and Epiphanies*, London 1962, pp. 164–75.

LINKLATER, ERIC: "Evelyn Waugh," in *The Art of Adventure*, London 1948, pp. 44–58.

LODGE, DAVID: *Catholic Fiction Since the Oxford Movement: Its Literary Form and Religious Content*, (unpublished M.A. thesis, London 1959).

MACAULAY, ROSE: "Evelyn Waugh," in *Writers of Today*, Second Series, ed. by Denys Val Baker, London 1948, pp. 135–51.

MARCUS, STEVEN: "Evelyn Waugh and the Art of Entertainment," in *Partisan Review*, XXIII, 1956, pp. 348-57.

MARTIN, GRAHAM: "Novelists of Three Decades: Evelyn Waugh, Graham Greene, C. P. Snow," in *The Pelican Guide to English Literature*, VII, The Modern Age, ed. by Boris Ford, London 1961, pp. 394–414.

O'DONNELL, DONAT (Conor Cruise O'Brien): *Maria Cross, Imaginative Patterns in a Group of Modern Catholic Writers*, London 1953.

O'FAOLAIN, SEAN: *The Vanishing Hero, Studies in the Novels of the Twenties*, London 1951.

SAVAGE, D. S.: "The Innocence of Evelyn Waugh," in *Focus Four: The Novelist As Thinker*, ed. by B. Rajan, London 1947, pp. 33–46.

SPENDER, STEPHEN: *The Creative Element, A Study of Vision, Despair and Orthodoxy among some Modern Writers*, London 1953.

STOPP, FREDERICK J.: *Evelyn Waugh: Portrait of an Artist*, London 1958. "Grace in Reins, Reflections on Mr. Waugh's *Brideshead* and *Helena*," in *The Month*, n.s., x, 1953, pp. 69–84. "The Circle and the Tangent, An Interpretation of Mr. Waugh's *Men at Arms*," in *The Month*, n.s., XII, 1954, pp. 18–34. "Waugh: End of an Illusion," in *Renascence*, IX, 1956, pp. 59–67, 76.

TOYNBEE, PHILIP: "Evelyn Waugh: Mourner for a World that Never Was," in *The Observer*, No. 8,887 (29 Oct. 1961), p. 21.

VOORHEES, RICHARD J.: "Evelyn Waugh Revisited," in *South Atlantic Quarterly*, XLVIII, 1949, pp. 270–80.

WALL, BARBARA: "Critics and Evelyn Waugh," in *America*, LXXVII, 1947, p. 354.

WECTER, DIXON: "On Dying in Southern California," in *The Pacific Spectator*, II, 1948, pp. 375–87.

WEST, REBECCA: *Ending in Earnest*, New York 1931.

WILSON, EDMUND: "Never Apologize, Never Explain: The Art of Evelyn Waugh," and "Splendors and Miseries of Evelyn Waugh," in *Classics and Commercials*; A Literary Chronicle of the Forties, New York 1950 and London, 1951, pp. 140–46 and 298–305.

WOODCOCK, GEORGE: "Evelyn Waugh: The Man and his Work," in *World Review*, n.s., I, 1949, pp. 51–56.